St. Thomas Aqu

By Da

M000119684

ISBN-13: 978-0692687567
ISBN: 0692687564

Cover and Interior by iAmplify.com.

Printed in the United States of America
Acid-free paper for permanence and durability

To Paula, Ena, Maura and Patrick

May your lives be a joyful search for He Who Is

TABLE OF CONTENTS

INTRODUCTION

I once asked a wise, old Dominican priest friend to sum up the teaching of St. Thomas Aquinas in as few words as possible. He needed only one. 'Nature,' he said.

It was years later, after much study of St. Thomas Aquinas, that I came to fully understand the meaning of his answer. St. Thomas' writings and especially his masterpiece, the *Summa Theologica*, assist man in his journey from God back to God. We are created by God and our lives can be a fascinating journey back to Him. And to be successful, we must understand who we are as human beings and our relationship with the rest of creation and our Creator. We must also know the final goal and purpose of our lives and how we can best accomplish it. Simply put, this requires that we become experts on human nature.

It is this journey that serves as the subject of this book of lessons. If you have a burning desire to come to know the God to Whom you are journeying, I think you will enjoy these lessons, activities and outdoor adventures. Ardently seeking God in our daily activities is what makes life an exciting adventure. Why not commit today to making each day of the rest of your life an intentional quest to come to know the very God who is your ultimate happiness and final destination?

If this interests you, I challenge you to pick up this book, read through the lessons slowly, either by yourself or with others, and allow the Angelic Doctor, St. Thomas Aquinas, to teach you how to make straight this journey to our loving God. These lessons will help train you to see life through a different lens, a much more beautiful and exciting lens. Will you allow God to sweep you off your feet?

In these lessons you will learn how to practice a 'spirituality of awareness.' This means learning to live with a mind and heart open to being amazed, allowing God to reveal Himself every moment of every day. It means never again experiencing one of God's creatures, like a butterfly or sparrow or a fellow human being, without being drawn to contemplate their Cause and Creator, the One who has brought these creatures into being and holds them in existence.

My prayers are with you as you begin this exciting journey. I hope this book of lessons helps you draw closer to Him who is eager to be found.

How To Use This Book

Each of the thirty lessons in this book contains six parts: an introductory section, a brief quote by St. Thomas Aquinas' *Summa Theologica*, a Fun Activity for Children based on the lesson, an Outside Adventure, an Awe and Wonder reflection, and a brief concluding prayer.

I recommend you start by reading the introductory section first alone and then a second time with your child or children if you are a parent or teacher. Be sure that everyone understands the main point of the lesson. Take time to discuss it if necessary. Next, I challenge you to read St. Thomas' own words from the *Summa Theologica*. Sometimes it's tough to read St. Thomas' writing, but it's beneficial to do this to see how this great saint organizes his thoughts and teachings. The more of his writing you read, the easier it gets!

If your children are young or young at heart, go on to complete the Fun Activity for Children and then move on to the Outdoor Adventure which is designed to get everyone outdoors, with God's creation, experiencing nature firsthand, away from electronics and other distractions. The Awe and Wonder section will help draw your mind to the beauty and grandeur of God and His creation. Finally, a brief prayer is said to focus our minds and hearts on thankfulness to God for Who He is and what we've learned in the lesson.

Feel free to read some or all of the parts of each lesson. Each person will find different sections more beneficial than others. It's hoped that after completing a lesson, a lively discussion will follow based on what was learned.

Reading St. Thomas' *Summa Theologica*

Each of the lessons from this book contains a brief excerpt from St. Thomas' masterpiece, the *Summa Theologica*. I used the translation from the Fathers of the English Dominican Province published by Christian Classics in Allen, TX. Each citation has an endnote reference found on page 153 so that you can easily find each quote in the *Summa* if you so desire.

I hope that this book of lessons inspires you to be interested in studying the *Summa Theologica* in greater depth. The *Summa* is contained in five volumes and is comprised of a total of 631 questions and approximately 3,000 articles. Each article begins with objections to St. Thomas' opinion on the topic. Following the objections is the 'Sed Contra' or 'On the Contrary' section where St. Thomas provides a quote from an authority to lend credibility to his opinion and teaching on the particular question. Next is the Corpus which contains the main body of St. Thomas' argument. The Corpus is followed by separate responses to each of the objections from the beginning of the article.

The *Summa Theologica* can be found in its entirety free of charge online and can be purchased in paperback relatively inexpensively. Reading the *Summa* has made a tremendous difference in my life and has helped me to see the world in a new and exciting way. I hope it has a similar effect on you.

LESSON 1

The Big Question: Where Am I Going?

Just about every moment of every day we are going somewhere. We go to church, to school, and to the grocery store. We go to sports games and parties. We're always on the move! But where are we going ultimately? In other words, as St. Thomas would ask, what is our final end?

St. Thomas teaches that our final end is something that we can never figure out on our own with the use of our natural reason. It's because our final end is 'too big' for our minds to fully understand in this life. In order for us to know the ultimate purpose of our lives, God has to reveal it to us. He does this first by sharing Divine mysteries that help us better understand the meaning of our lives and our destiny. St. Thomas Aquinas calls these mysteries Sacred Doctrine. They Include teachings such as the existence of the Holy Trinity, three Persons in one God, and the reality of heaven and hell. It's necessary that God reveal these mysteries so that we can direct our lives to attaining our final end. Without this knowledge, our lives would lack purpose, and we would have no idea what we are supposed to do to achieve our end because it would remain unrevealed.

What then should be our final end? It's a state of perfect knowledge of God. In other words, knowing God will make us perfectly happy. But God is a mystery and we can't fully know Him in this life. So in addition to Sacred Doctrine, God has left many clues about Himself for us to find in this life if we're paying attention and being observant. All the lessons in this book will help us learn how to come to know God as best possible here on earth in preparation for knowing Him more fully one day in heaven.

ST. THOMAS SAYS...

It was necessary for man's salvation that there should be a knowledge revealed by God besides philosophical science built up by human reason. Firstly, indeed, because man is directed to God, as to an end that surpasses the grasp of his reason. But the end must first be known by men who are to direct their thoughts and actions to the end. Hence it was necessary for the salvation of man that certain truths which exceed human reason should be made known to him by divine revelation.

FUN ACTIVITY FOR CHILDREN

This game will require at least three players (the more the better!) and someone to serve as the facilitator. Ideally the players will be children and an adult will be the facilitator.

Each of the players should write down three unique things about himself or herself that they think most or all of the other players don't know. Examples could include their favorite restaurant or the country they'd most like to visit, or that they once found a snake in their closet. Anything is fair game as long as it's true.

Once all the players have written down their three facts about themselves, they should hand their list to the facilitator, who should scramble them and write them all down on a separate piece of paper. So if five children are playing, the facilitator will have a list of fifteen things in random order.

The facilitator next slowly reads each of the facts while giving each player time to write down who they think wrote each of the clues. So if five people are playing, each player will have a list of fifteen guesses based on the clues. Of course three of the clues will be their own.

After all the clues have been read, the facilitator can go back and read each of the clues again, allowing the person for each to identify himself or herself. Everyone gets a point for each correct answer.

When finished, see if everyone can work out how this activity applies to the lesson.

OUTSIDE ADVENTURE

Go outside some clear night when the stars are visible. Ask each child to observe the stars in the sky and see if they can imagine any groups of stars that look like things with which they are familiar. For example, one child may see the design of a horse or a smiley face or a dinosaur in a particular group of stars. Each child should write down up to five things that he or she sees in the stars. Afterwards, have them compare their list with the other children to see if anyone saw the same thing.

Let this lead into a discussion about the mystery of outer space. Ask them if they've ever wondered how many stars are up in the sky or how many galaxies are in outer space? The truth is that scientists have no sure answer to either of these questions. Scientists estimate that there are up to 170,000,000,000 (that's 170 billion) galaxies, and as many as 1,000,000,000,000,000,000,000,000 (that's a septillion) stars in the sky and outer space. But no one knows for sure. Does outer space go on forever or does it end somewhere? Despite our many advances in science and technology, there are still far more things that we don't know compared to what we do know.

What does this tell us about ourselves, our nature, and our God? In light of what we've learned in this lesson so far, why might God allow many things in the world to reach beyond our understanding?

AWE AND WONDER

In the lessons that follow, we are going to spend time learning and contemplating many qualities and characteristics of God that exceed our ability to fully understand. Let's start with one that is utterly amazing. God is existence. Notice that I didn't write 'God exists' like we would say about ourselves (you exist and I exist). Rather, God is existence itself! Isn't that a mind-boggling statement? What does that mean to you?

Isn't it incredible to consider that God transcends our little minds' abilities to know Him perfectly? Did you know that if you could understand God in every way possible, then you would be God? He is awesome and unfathomable, but remember, we can come to know Him somewhat now and much better later if we are blessed to rest with Him in heaven.

PRAYER

My God, thank You for allowing me to contemplate things that surpass my limited reason, such as the existence of heaven and other mysteries of the faith. Please give me the humility to accept that there are many things that I cannot know without Your help.

LESSON 2

How Are We Able To Describe God?

We learned in the first lesson that some of the teachings about God and our final end surpass our natural ability to fully understand. But this seems to create a dilemma. If God and heaven and other supernatural realities are so high and lofty, so out of reach for us mere human beings to fully comprehend, then can we come to know Him or anything else beyond us through the use of our reason? How then are we to come to know anything about Him during this life?

It's important to understand the role of metaphors, analogies and similes in coming to know God and other mysteries of our faith. Metaphors and analogies are used to compare two seemingly different things in order to show how they resemble each other in some way. Similes compare two things using the words 'like' or 'as.' Metaphors, analogies and similes can be used to help us come to know things that are mysterious and unfathomable, like God Himself, by using words and things that we understand from our human experience. Since God is so far beyond us, we make use of what we can know in order to better understand and describe God. In Scripture, for example, God is compared to rocks and lions and water and other such things with which we are familiar. Because we can't know Him directly due to the limitations of our human nature, we must, in a sense, bring Him down to our level, at least in the way we speak about Him.

ST. THOMAS SAYS...

It is befitting Holy Writ to put forward divine and spiritual truths by means of comparisons with material things. For God provides for everything according to the capacity of its nature. Now it is natural to man to attain to intellectual truths through sensible objects, because all our knowledge originates from sense. Hence in Holy Writ, spiritual truths are fittingly taught under the likeness of material things. This is what Dionysius says: "We cannot be enlightened by the divine rays except they be hidden within the covering of many sacred veils."

FUN ACTIVITY FOR CHILDREN

Draw a picture of yourself, making sure to include your eyes, nose, ears, mouth and hands in the drawing. For each of these five body parts, which represent our five senses (sight, smell, hearing, taste and touch), list three things that you have come to know about the world through the use of that particular sense. For example, you could list the blue sky under 'eye' because you learned about it through the use of your sight. You came to know the delicious taste of ice cream through the use of your tongue (mouth) and the sense of taste. Now it's your turn to think of three original things that you've learned through each of your five senses.

Next, try to think of anything that you've learned about the created world apart from your five senses. Can you think of anything?

18

How does this activity help us understand the main point of this lesson?

OUTSIDE ADVENTURE

In this activity we're going to learn to pay attention to the use of our senses in the activities of our daily life. Get a notepad or journal and write down the names of your five senses: sight, smell, hearing, taste and touch. Next, go outside and see what kind of things you can find in the natural world that correspond to the five senses. Some will be easy, such as sight, because you'll likely see many beautiful things such as birds and trees and sunsets. Others, like taste, will be more challenging. But maybe you have a garden outside and your parents will let you pick something and eat it, or there might be other things you can safely taste outdoors, like an apple or pear on a tree.

See if you can smell a rose or the aroma of a neighbor cooking out on their grill, listen to the birds singing joyfully, touch your pet dog's fur or the rough bark of a tree. Make a log of all the things you consciously experienced through the use of your five senses.

Afterwards, talk about how these things can help you to better understand and appreciate God.

AWE AND WONDER

If you were to look at a list of all the metaphors used in Sacred Scripture to describe God, the list would be long and filled with many familiar words. Here are just a few of the metaphors that would be on that list: Rock, Lion, Wind, Breath, Vine, Light, Fountain, Gate, Water, Bread and Fire. Many of these are part of our daily experience. Others might create impressions in our mind, such as the strong lion as the 'king of the jungle' or the rock for its heavy weight and immovableness. Many seem to have little in common with each other, like a fountain and bread. So what are we to make of all these words which God has chosen to describe Himself in the Bible? Aren't they all things that we've come to know through the use of our five senses, and doesn't each teach us something about our great God?

PRAYER

My God, I love You and am thankful that I can come to know You through the things on earth that I can experience with the use of my senses. I desire to know You better each day.

LESSON 3

Can God's Existence Be Demonstrated?

Now that we've learned about metaphors, analogies and similes as important ways that we, as rational creatures, can come to know God, it's our task to consider whether we are ever able to know with any certainty that God does in fact exist. In the *Summa Theologica*, St. Thomas doesn't just assume that God exists. Rather, He explains the proofs for His existence. Remember, we learned in Lesson 1 that the purpose of our lives is to rest in perfect knowledge of our great God in heaven. But we also learned that heaven and God Himself cannot be fully understood with our natural, human ability. But in this lesson, we'll learn that there are some things about God that we can come to know through the use of our reason and senses in our daily experiences.

Every day we come across what St. Thomas calls 'traces' of God. But we need to be reminded and trained to pay attention because it's all too easy to get distracted and never take notice of all the divine clues that surround us. We see stars and daffodils and babies and bumblebees and countless other amazing creatures every day. All these should be considered 'effects.' And every effect must have a cause. We need to become increasingly aware that the ultimate cause of all these beautiful creatures we experience every day is none other than God. Let's begin training ourselves to understand that God is the designer, architect and artist of this masterpiece we call our world, and the myriad of creatures that inhabit it. Let's begin to pay closer attention to all the beauty that surrounds us and trace it all to its Cause.

ST. THOMAS SAYS...

When an effect is better known to us than its cause, from the effect we proceed to the knowledge of the cause. And from every effect the existence of its proper cause can be demonstrated, so long as its effects are better known to us; because since every effect depends upon its cause, if the effect exists, the cause must pre-exist. Hence the existence of God, insofar as it is not self-evident to us, can be demonstrated from those of His effects which are known to us.

FUN ACTIVITY FOR CHILDREN

Have you ever played indoor bowling? Get ten small (approximately 16 oz.) water bottles from the store and put them at the end of a hallway or room in the way you'd see at the bowling alley (four in the back row, then a row of three, a row of two and one in the front). Next, get a soccer ball or basketball (or a similar sized ball), stand back about ten to twenty feet and roll the ball toward the 'bowling pins' to see how many you can knock over. Let each child give it a try. Afterwards, talk about how this activity demonstrates the relationship between cause and effect.

See if you can also think of other cause and effect relationships from your daily life.

Examples of effects that lead to an understanding of causes include hearing the doorbell ring or a knock on the door (the effect) and knowing that someone (the cause) has arrived at the house. Another example is smelling a wonderful aroma coming from the kitchen (effect) and knowing that mom (cause) has just cooked a tasty meal.

Examples of cause to effect relationships include seeing a dark ominous cloud outside (cause) and knowing that rain (effect) will soon fall. Another example is hearing someone tell a funny joke (cause) and knowing that laughter (effect) will follow.

Now it's your turn to think of a few original examples of Effect-Cause and Cause-Effect relationships.

What do these have to do with demonstrating the existence of God?

OUTSIDE ADVENTURE

Let's go outside and see how easy it is to associate this lesson with outdoor activities that we do just about every day. It will be clear that just about everything you do when you play outdoors involves examples of cause and effect.

One such fun activity is a simple game of kickball or soccer. Think about the foot (cause) making contact with the kickball and it flying into the outfield (effect). Notice how when you move your legs faster (cause), your running speed increases (effect). When

23

someone scores a goal (effect) in soccer, you know that the ball somehow was moved into the net by someone's foot (cause). If the weather permits, fill up some balloons with water and let everyone have a good old-fashioned water balloon fight in the yard. You'll certainly be able to identify a lot of fun causes and effects in that game!

Think of other games that you play regularly and how each has examples of causes and effects and talk about how these games can be good opportunities to talk about God as the ultimate Cause of everything we experience and enjoy every day.

AWE AND WONDER

Think of a small child who discovers something for the first time, like a little bug crawling across the room or a light switch that 'magically' turns a light on in the house. Notice how the child will watch it with amazement for a long time and then might want to do it over and over again! Little children are rarely bored because they have a natural sense of awe and wonder with the experiences of their daily lives. All things are new and fresh to a child. They've not lived long enough to become jaded or bored by excessive living of days or repeated experiences. Can you bring yourself back to remembering how it felt to be little, when everything was new and fresh and exciting? Do you remember those days when you could watch a minnow in the creek or see a star in the sky and be absolutely blown away with amazement? Can we rediscover this sense of awe and connect it with sincere thanksgiving to the One Who is the source of all the beauty in our lives?

PRAYER

My God, thank you for all the wonders of creation that surround me. Help me to regain and never again lose a child-like amazement for my daily experiences of the world.

LESSON 4

Can We Prove That God Exists?

In the last lesson, we discovered that it's possible to come to know God as the Cause and Creator of the world by simply observing the natural world around us (the effects) and applying our God-given gift of reason and our senses to trace them back to their causes and ultimately the Cause of all causes. Let's spend one more lesson focusing on proving that God exists before we begin learning about His specific attributes.

Notice that just because we can prove that God exists doesn't mean that we know very much about Him. In this lesson we will focus on what is undoubtedly the most talked about and popular article in the entire *Summa Theologica*: namely, the proofs for the existence of God. St. Thomas proves that God exists five different ways using reason rather than religious beliefs based on faith. In this lesson we will focus on only one of these 'Five Ways,' as they're often called. The other four proofs will be explained in future lessons in this book.

The first proof is based on an observation of the way many creatures in the world behave in their daily activities. We learned in the last lesson that God is the Divine Artist responsible for countless effects that we experience every day. In regard to irrational animals, those creatures that lack intelligence such as dogs, horses, flies and grasshoppers, we often hear references to 'instinct' to describe the predictable way these creatures behave. Ants predictably build mounds and ducks predictably fly south in the winter, and salmon predictably swim upstream to spawn. But who is the author of these instinctive behaviors if these creatures are not 'smart enough' to know what they are doing? We should ask that if these animals, lacking intelligence, act in certain predictable ways, for a clear and certain end, then who is 'pulling the strings,' so to speak?

ST. THOMAS SAYS...

The fifth way is taken from the governance of the world. We see that things which lack intelligence, such as natural bodies, act for an end, and this is evident from their acting always, or nearly always, in the same way, so as to obtain the best result. Hence it is plain that not fortuitously, but designedly, do they achieve their end. Now whatever lacks intelligence cannot move towards an end, unless it be directed by some being endowed with knowledge and intelligence; as the arrow is shot to its mark by the archer. Therefore some intelligent being exists by whom all natural things are directed to their end; and this being we call God.

FUN ACTIVITY FOR CHILDREN

Before this activity be sure each child understands what is meant by 'instinct' as related to animals in the world. Ask each child to think of one original example of an 'instinct' in animals, and either keep it in their mind or write it down, but keep it a secret from the others playing the game. They'll need to be sure to think of (and write down) not only the name of the animal but what it does that is commonly considered an instinct. Several examples were provided in the previous section of this lesson. See if they can think of others.

Next, one child should begin drawing his or her animal and action on paper in full view of the others who are participating. The goal is for the others to guess what animal and action the child is drawing. After someone in the group guesses both the animal and the activity correctly, have another child do the same.

This game can either be just for fun or it can be turned into a competition. For example, you can time how long it takes for each child to have his or her drawing Identified correctly and you can also award points for the person who guesses it correctly.

OUTSIDE ADVENTURE

Let's go outside and spend some time observing some examples of the beautiful order of the natural world. Give each child a notepad or piece of paper and a pen and see how quickly (If you want to make it a competition) they can find five examples of 'instincts' in animals or creatures of any sort. Remind the children that this simply means the creature lacks intelligence but still acts for an end. So this can include not only birds, ants, and fish but also trees and flowers and even grass! If the parents don't mind, let the kids dig around in the dirt or lift up rocks to see what kind of creatures they can find. Extra credit for the most original examples of 'instinct' in the natural world!

Hopefully a fun conversation will follow about Who truly is the author of what is referred to as instinct in the natural world. Doesn't every plant, insect, animal, and even planet move and behave in such a way as is best for its own survival and the good of the whole universe? Hopefully this will provide you a sense of peace knowing 'Someone' has everything under control.

AWE AND WONDER

I've heard it referred to as some kind of magic trick. It's an incredible natural process common to gardeners and farmers called 'composting.' First you collect leftover vegetable and fruit waste like banana peels, cantaloupe rinds and mushroom stalks, egg shells, coffee grounds, tea bags and grass cuttings. Then you put these in a compost pile outside and in as little as a month you will see this pile of waste products transformed into nutrient-rich soil perfect for your garden or yard. So how does this happen? Well, microbes, bacteria, worms, snails, insects and fungi get working on the waste products, 'instinctively' working together to turn something worthless into something very valuable. Each of these creatures plays a very important role in the composting process. And as you can likely guess, this is no magic trick at all. It's a wonderful example of the beauty of our world under the direction of our great God who orders all things for the benefit of the whole universe.

PRAYER

My God, please help me to pay more attention to the small details of Your creation and be filled with amazement by the perfection, beauty and order of the world You have created.

LESSON 5

Is God Simple or Complicated?

By now you've likely discovered a new sense of awe for God and His creation, as you contemplate in a fresh way His many wonders and the world He has created. We now begin a series of lessons designed to describe, as best possible, God's nature and his various attributes. It's the same God who is the great Cause of the many effects we are learning to notice, the same God whom we desire to know and love eternally in heaven. Let's try to awake each day desiring to better know this incredible God, believing that we can experience Him profoundly each day.

Do you think God is simple or complicated? In some ways it seems He is complicated because He has to know so much, answer so many prayers, and be everywhere in the world at the same time. So it may come as a surprise that St. Thomas teaches that far from being complicated, God is perfectly simple and it's we human beings that are much more complicated. So what makes God so simple?

His simplicity is based more on what He isn't rather than what He is and what He doesn't have rather than what He has. For example, God Is pure Spirit and therefore has no body and no parts and He was not caused by anyone or anything. He can't be acted upon and He is not limited in space. God is the Uncaused Cause, which is the second of our five proofs for the existence of God. Everything in the world has a cause, as we learned in a previous lesson, and this cause also must have a cause and that cause must have a cause. But we can't go back forever in regard to causes. There must have existed from all time one Being that does not have a cause but is rather uncaused and the Cause of all other things. And this is God, the Uncaused Cause.

ST. THOMAS SAYS...

The absolute simplicity of God may be shown in many ways. First, there is neither composition of quantitative parts in God, since He is not a body; nor composition of matter and form; His essence does not differ from His existence; neither is there in Him composition of genus and difference, nor of subject and accident. Therefore, it is clear that God is nowise composite, but is altogether simple. Secondly, because every composite is posterior to its component parts, and is dependent on them; but God is the first being. Thirdly, because every composite has a cause, for things in themselves different cannot unite unless something causes them to unite. But God is uncaused, since he is the first efficient cause. Fourthly, because in every composite there must be potentiality and actuality; but this does not apply to God.

FUN ACTIVITY FOR CHILDREN

Since this lesson is about the simplicity of God we're going to do a simple activity!

Get some bubbles that have a wand through which the children can blow to create bubbles. See who can blow the biggest bubble or the most bubbles with one blow. See whose bubble can be kept 'alive' for the longest in the air without popping, by blowing underneath it to keep it suspended. You can likely think of many other fun activities that can be done with bubbles!

Now here's the fun part. Try to list some of the differences between a bubble and God based on all that we've learned in this lesson. I'll provide one and you try to come up with some others. The bubble was created by the child using the wand and his or her blowing, right? At one time the bubble didn't exist and another moment it did. That means it had to have come into existence by someone or something else. God is not created so that would be one difference between God and the bubble!

Now it's your turn. What other differences can you find between the bubble and God?

OUTSIDE ADVENTURE

One of the ways that we can come to know God through an observation of His created world is to notice not only how creatures are like God but also how they are unlike Him. Remember we learned that God is bigger than our minds can imagine so therefore in many ways He's different from His created world.

Go outside somewhere interesting, like a park down the street or a nearby creek where you can go to observe some creatures in nature. Pay attention to the creatures and notice how they look and behave. Next, based on this lesson on God's simplicity, either write down or discuss how these creatures are not like God.

One example could be that whatever you see has a body or material of some sort, and we've learned that God doesn't have a body or anything perceptible to the senses. There are many other examples. See if you can think of others and let this begin a discussion on God's simplicity.

AWE AND WONDER

Can you imagine yourself without a body, without movement and having never been created? It's almost impossible to do because these are parts of our nature. But what if our body was gone and there was no more moving from one place to another, no more eating and drinking, no more sleeping and waking up? If you can imagine this, you will be able to understand one of the qualities of God: namely, His simplicity.

But did you know that the souls of most all of the faithful departed who have died and are now in heaven are what's called 'separated souls?' That means they have souls but no bodies. We'll learn a lot more about separated souls in the next book, but you should know that even though they're in heaven they miss having their bodies. That's because our bodies are beautiful and a necessary part of our human nature, both in heaven and on earth. It's not natural for our souls to be separated from our bodies. Remember we learned in a previous lesson that we come to know about God through our senses, which are a very important part of our bodies.

PRAYER

My Lord, I know I cannot fully understand You while here on earth, but help me to have a greater desire to know You and Your nature through daily prayer and study. Help me to understand You as being perfectly simple.

LESSON 6

Is God Perfect?

While God's simplicity may be difficult for us to understand, the idea of perfection is likely a little easier to grasp. We've all experienced things that we consider to be perfect or close to being perfect. Maybe you've had a (nearly) perfect friend or you've gotten a perfect score on a test, or you've witnessed a perfect sunset, or felt a perfect, gentle breeze on your face. Maybe you've tried to reach a certain level of perfection in a sport or some other activity. In fact, our being able to recognize that some things are more perfect than others relates to the third of St. Thomas' proof for the existence of God. In order for us to notice degrees of perfection in the created world it follows that there must be an ultimate standard of perfection for all things and this standard is God Himself.

But what does it mean to say that God is perfect? It's not that He's perfect in one particular way, but rather that He is perfect in everything. Perfectly perfect!

Every perfection that we experience in this life is a reflection (and participation) of the absolute perfection of God, because for something on earth to be perfect, it is first a perfection existing in God. Any effect must exist first in its cause, and God is the cause of all things, so everything exists in Him.

Because it's impossible for us to comprehend God's perfection, we can learn about Him through those things that we can understand such as our experiences of His creation that participate in His ultimate perfection.

ST. THOMAS SAYS...

All created perfections are in God. Hence He is spoken of as universally perfect, because He lacks not any excellence which may be found in any genus....because whatever perfection exists in an effect must be found in the effective cause: either in the same formality—as when man reproduces man; or in a more eminent degree—thus in the sun is the likeness of whatever is generated by the sun's power. Since therefore God is the first effective cause of things, the perfections of all things must pre-exist in God in a more eminent way.

FUN ACTIVITY FOR CHILDREN

Have each of the children come up with five unique questions that he or she will ask the others who are playing the game. They can be of any type they'd like, such as trivia questions about history or science or about issues having to do with Scripture or other aspects of the faith, or something interesting he or she learned in school recently. The child must know the answer and it should be something that would be possible for the others to know.

Each child should then take turns asking the others his or her five questions on the quiz. Each of the other children should write down their answers on a separate piece of paper. When finished, the child who made the quiz should award each player a grade either as a percentage or how many were correct out of a possible five correct.

Did any of the players get a perfect score? If not, how close did each get to being perfect on the quiz? Discuss the relationship between this quiz and God's perfection as explained above.

OUTSIDE ADVENTURE

This activity will be best done with a magnifying glass or even a microscope if one is available. If neither are available, the naked eye will be just fine.

Go outside and see if you can find some little critters such as an ant, a cricket, a lady bug or a termite. The smaller the creature the better. Next, use the magnifying glass or microscope to see the precise features of the creature that you've found. Look at the fine details of their eyes, legs, antennae, etc. and take note of how intricately designed is each of its features. Is there anything about their design that surprises you or that you've never noticed before? Keep in mind while studying the little creature that it is the result of a master artist who is clearly detail-oriented!

If you feel ambitious you can go on to do further research on the anatomy of the particular creature you've found. Hopefully this activity will lead to a fun discussion on the perfection of creatures and their relationship to the Author of all perfection.

AWE AND WONDER

Have you ever been bitten by a mosquito? If they exist where you live, then most likely you have been the victim of one of these critters. Most people see them as nothing more than nuisances and for good reason. They do suck blood and can also carry a number of diseases. But consider how intricately designed is the mosquito.

Did you know that the mosquito's head is filled with sensory equipment that helps guide it to people and animals? The mosquito has two large compound eyes, each with tiny lenses that are capable of detecting the smallest movement and variations in light. The mosquito has long, feathery antennae that contain sensitive receptors that are capable of detecting carbon dioxide in human breath from more than 100 feet away. Is it not amazing that this little creature, which we find to be no more than an annoyance, is so beautifully and intentionally made? Each one is created perfectly with amazing detail and specificity. Consider how much attention and detail goes into the creation of every single one of God's creatures!

PRAYER

Lord, help me understand that any perfection I experience in life is a reflection of Your absolute perfection. Please help me draw closer to You through my attraction to the good and beautiful things that participate in Your perfection.

LESSON 7

Are All of God's Creature's Good?

We've now learned that God is absolutely simple and He's perfect in every way, and contains in Himself all perfection that exists in His creatures (even the mosquito!). In this lesson we will learn that everything God creates is good and has in some way perfection in its being. And this has more to do with God than it does with His creatures. The goodness of God's creatures is a reflection of the One who creates them.

Our great God creates only that which is good because He is Goodness itself, and nothing bad or defiled can come from perfect Goodness. If God could create something bad or evil, this would be a contradiction because He would no longer be perfectly good, right? This is an example of the inherent optimism of Christianity. We worship an absolutely good God, and therefore we hold in great esteem all of His creatures, since they all reflect in some way His infinite goodness and beauty. You might be surprised to hear that even the devil, the prince of evil and the father of lies, was created good (in fact very good... remember the name 'Lucifer' means 'to shine' or 'to bear light'). Knowing that all created things are good will hopefully change the way we view the world and all of God's creatures that we encounter each day. And It will hopefully instill In us a great sense of gratitude for the One who has blessed us with so many such gifts!

ST. THOMAS SAYS...

Every being, as being, is good. For all being, as being, has actuality and is in some way perfect; since every act implies some sort of perfection; and perfection implies desirability and goodness. Hence it follows that every being as such is good. No being can be spoken of as evil, formally as being, but only so far as it lacks being.

FUN ACTIVITY FOR CHILDREN

Search around your home for five different things that were made by a human being (or human beings). I'm sure there are countless such items that you can find, such as a pair of scissors, a broom, a plastic cup or a radio. Often we take such things for granted because we can just drive to the store and purchase them without giving much consideration to the fact that someone designed and constructed them. Once you've identified your five items, consider the answers to the questions below and discuss them with the others in your group or family.

1. For what purpose was it made?

2. What is good about it?

3. What does its goodness tell us about the person or persons who created it?

4. How does this activity relate to this lesson?

OUTSIDE ADVENTURE

This activity will require participants to challenge the very point of this lesson, that all things created by God are good. As a group, come up with a list of up to ten creatures or things that you would consider to be 'bad.' Be sure that some or all of the things on your list are able to be found nearby where you live. Be creative and you'll likely be able to think of many things that fit this description. Ideas can include spiders, termites, fire ants, wasps, thorns on roses and poison Ivy. Now it's your turn to come up with your own list of ten 'bad' creatures in the natural world.

Next, take your list outside and see how many examples from the list you can find as a group.

** This clearly requires prudence and good judgment. Never put yourself in danger by trying to find poisonous snakes or spiders or anything that can cause you harm. Be sure also that this is done only with the permission and supervision of a parent or another adult. **

After the activity, do some research to see what is good about each of these creatures on your list. Are any of them truly bad or is there some way that each is in fact good?

AWE AND WONDER

Have you ever taken the time to thank God for everything in your life? Literally everything? We are surrounded by goodness every moment, every day of our lives, and yet we often are blinded to this fact. Do we see the goodness in a blade of grass or a tree or a bumblebee? And most importantly, do we thank God for the people in our lives, such as our parents, siblings and friends? Can we take a few minutes of our day today to recognize the beauty of God's creation and see goodness in everything?

We've all heard the advice to stop and smell the roses. Have you ever done it? Do you ever stop and take notice of the gifts God has poured down upon us, most especially in the people whom we encounter each day? Human beings are good and beautiful in a most significant way. We were created to God's image and likeness. As we learned above, we can find good even in creatures that can potentially harm us if we see these creatures in light of their purpose in the 'big picture' of God's creation.

PRAYER

God, please help me to take notice of the goodness that surrounds me at every moment in my life and to trace that goodness to You as its Origin, Source and Cause.

LESSON 8

How Are Creatures Related to God?

In light of the previous lesson on the goodness of all of God's creatures, you might ask yourself why God fills the world with countless small reminders of Himself, even though they lack the fullness of goodness and perfection which is God Himself?

The reason is that by being attracted to these many good things which God has created, we are actually being drawn to God Himself, Who is the Creator and Perfection of the goodness represented by these many creatures. We are drawn to created things because we ultimately desire and long for God as our final end. This is what it means to say that goodness has an aspect of a final cause, or we could even say that goodness has an aspect of THE Final Cause, God Himself. When we find ourselves drawn to the goodness of a creature of any sort, we should realize that this attraction we are experiencing is a gentle pull from our loving God, who has placed a portion of His goodness in that to which we are attracted. Just think of all the things you are attracted to each day, from delicious food and drinks to friends and sports and other activities. Can you see how each of these can be connected to our good God?

ST. THOMAS SAYS...

Since goodness is that which all things desire, and since this has the aspect of an end, it is clear that goodness implies the aspect of an end. Nevertheless, the idea of goodness presupposes the idea of an efficient cause, and also of a formal cause.

FUN ACTIVITY FOR CHILDREN

Ask each child or participant in the activity to think about their favorite book, movie, song or other piece of art (like a painting or sculpture). Next write three of these down but don't share the information with anyone else for now.

Next, one at a time each child should act out his or her book, movie, song or art for the others without using words or sounds of any sort (like charades). Keep track of how long it takes someone to guess what is being acted out and also write down who guesses correctly. See also who can guess the names of the producer of the movies, the author of the books or the singer of the songs for each charade. Have a prize for the winners if you'd like.

During the game see if you can have a conversation about the connection between this game and this lesson? The hint is that you should discuss the connection between the works of art and their creators (authors, producers, singers) in light of the point of the lesson.

OUTSIDE ADVENTURE

Remember in the previous lesson when we found things in the home that were made by human beings and wrote down what was good about each? Now that you're outside, find a few things to which you find yourself attracted. You might want to consider starting a 'goodness journal' of things you see that are beautiful and good. Some of the things you notice will be natural, such as a beautiful flower, a running stream or a tree you'd like to climb. Others might be man-made, like a trampoline, a swimming pool or even an ice cream cone. The key here is to recognize goodness everywhere you look, both in natural (God-made) things and artificial (man-made) things.

Notice how it feels to be attracted to each of these things and realize that you desire them because of something good in them. Consciously make the connection between that which is good and its creator (or Creator). Can you see that in every case you are also experiencing a gentle tug toward a loving and good God who is the Creator of all that is good? Can you see how doing this will also make you more appreciative of the many blessings in your life, many of which you perhaps don't usually notice?

AWE AND WONDER

Do you know what is considered to be the most famous work of art of all time? It's generally believed to be the Mona Lisa painting by Leonardo da Vinci. It was painted in the early 16th century, and the painting is thought to have taken da Vinci up to 15 years to complete. It is now on permanent display at the Louvre Museum in Paris, France. An estimated six million people travel to the museum each year to view and study the painting. The enigmatic look on Mona Lisa's face is just one of the aspects of this painting that has fascinated people for centuries. When we see such a painting, we often desire to 'get into the mind' of the artist, to know why da Vinci drew it, and to find out what motivated him, what was his inspiration.

Let's practice taking this same sense of wonder to the natural world by taking some time today to sit quietly and reflect on something beautiful that you experience in nature. Practice making the connection between the art and the artist (God) and being thankful for the gift of this creation. Try to make this a daily habit.

PRAYER

My God, I desire to be drawn to You through my attraction to Your creatures. Please help me make the connection between these good things and their Source and Cause, You Who are perfect Goodness itself. All that I desire is a desire for You.

LESSON 9

Is God Everywhere?

Now we know that many of the good things we experience each day are intended to draw us to God as their Cause and Creator. It seems logical to ask now where God is and if He is in any way in all these good things to which we are attracted.

We always hear about God being in heaven, but what about all these things that are drawing us to Him (but aren't Him)? And in what way is God everywhere, as St. Thomas teaches? God is not the dog or the mockingbird or the rainbow or the tree or the kind person I met today, is He?

Here it's important to make the distinction between the Christian understanding of God being everywhere and the pantheistic belief of God being everything. These good things are not God, but He is present in each of them, holding them in existence and being. Without God 'being everywhere,' everything would cease to exist, because He is the supreme Principal and Cause of everything in the world. So if our goal is to come to know and love God and unite ourselves to Him, we need not look far to find Him!

ST. THOMAS SAYS...

(God) is in all things giving them being, power and operation; so He is in every place as giving it existence and locative power. Again, things placed are in place, inasmuch as they fill place; and God fills every place; not, indeed, like a body, for a body is said to fill place inasmuch as it excludes the co-presence of another body; whereas by God being in a place, others are not thereby excluded from it; indeed, by the very fact that He gives being to the things that fill every place, He Himself fills every place.

FUN ACTIVITY FOR CHILDREN

Find a volunteer to go first and provide him or her with a pen or pencil and a piece of paper. An adult should secretly give this child an idea of something to draw while the others guess what is being drawn. Examples would be something like 'pizza' or 'sail boat' or 'butterfly. But there is one stipulation. Once the pen touches the paper, it cannot be lifted until either someone guesses correctly or the drawing is finished.

If you'd like to make it a competition, see how long it takes for someone to guess the picture correctly and also keep track of who is the first to guess correctly. Each player can take turns drawing the pictures and everyone else guesses.

Once finished ask the children to think about how focused they were when drawing the pictures and making sure not to lift their pen. See if you can make the connection to God 'drawing' us and holding us in existence every moment of every day, never 'lifting His pen' but always consciously willing for us to be alive as His children.

OUTSIDE ADVENTURE

Let's get a group together outside and play a good old-fashioned game of hide and go seek. Set the boundaries and any rules you'd like for the game, and then pick teams and let one team hide while the other team searches for those who are hiding. If you'd like to make it a competition, see how long it takes for all members of each team to be located by members of the other team.

This is an example of how a simple game we've all played before can be used as a teaching tool to learn about the attributes of God. Isn't the whole point of hide and seek to get away from the other team, to find a secret place where hopefully they won't be able to find you?

Consider the point of this lesson: that God is everywhere, holding everything in being and existence every moment of every day. How does this relate to our game of hide and seek and what does this tell us about our relationship with God?

AWE AND WONDER

Most of us know the feeling of having one thing on our mind for a long time, something we're particularly interested in. Perhaps it's a dear friend whom we can't stop thinking about, or a pet dog or cat, or special gift that we're enamored with and can't get out of our mind. Or maybe we have thought about a particular food we crave or some other material good that we really desire and can't stop thinking about. But it's never the case that we MUST continue thinking about these things in order for them to continue to exist. Our thinking of them is not their cause and reason for existing.

Imagine if that was the case. What if your best friend or child or mom or dad only existed if you consistently thought about them, never for a moment taking your mind off of them? That would be some kind of pressure, right? Well, imagine how true this is for God, but instead of thinking of one thing lest it fall out of existence, He simultaneously 'thinks' about every creature in existence at every moment!

PRAYER

Lord, thank You for the gift of my life and for being present with me at every moment of every day. I know You are with me always and that You love and care for me. Help me to be more aware of Your presence each moment.

LESSON 10

Does God Ever Change?

In this lesson, we will learn that God is immutable. That is, He cannot change. Nothing changes with God, including His 'mind.' Remember, He's perfect so why would He want to change? It's difficult for us to understand this because change is a fundamental part of our lives. We get older. Our looks and thoughts change and we do different things every day. (Remember we are complicated, God is simple). But God, being perfectly simple, does not change. He acts and is never acted upon. Nothing 'happens' to God. And nothing we do changes God in any way, even our prayers (which we'll tackle in a future lesson). And unlike us, He never moves, which leads us to our fourth proof for God's existence. All things which move were moved by something else which was also moved by something else, but this can't go back forever. There must be an unmoved Mover who has never been acted upon but is responsible for moving all else. The Unmoved Mover is God Himself.

ST. THOMAS SAYS...

God is altogether immutable. First, because it was shown above that there is some first being, whom we call God; and that this first being must be pure act, without the admixture of any potentiality, for the reason that, absolutely, potentiality is posterior to act. Now everything which is in any way changed, is in some way in potentiality. Hence it is evident that it is impossible for God to be in any way changeable. Also, because everything which is moved acquires something by its movement, and attains to what it had not attained previously. But since God is infinite, comprehending in Himself all the plenitude of perfection of all being, He cannot acquire anything new, nor extend Himself to anything whereto He was not extended previously.

FUN ACTIVITY FOR CHILDREN

In this activity we're going to play a game that most kids are familiar with, but we're going to give it new meaning in light of this lesson. Have at least two children make themselves into the pose of a statue and see how long they can remain still without moving in any way (except very small movements like blinking eyes or breathing, etc.). Once someone moves any part of their body, he or she is eliminated from the game. The last one to be eliminated from the game is the winner! You can also do a similar game, seeing who can go the longest without smiling, laughing or blinking, using the same format as in the statue game.

These fun games allow the children to see just how much change and movement are part of their everyday lives, every moment of our day. It's very difficult for us not to move or change, isn't it? But God never changes and He never moves, so He'd be the champion of these games, right? (if only He had a body with which to play the game!)

OUTSIDE ADVENTURE

Have everyone go outside and anyone who wants to participate in the activity should bring a pen and paper. Have each child write the numbers 1-10 down the left margin of their paper.

Now, it's time for everyone to become very quiet so that all can pay close attention to their environment. Everyone should remain in close proximity, and each participant should write down ten things that they notice changing in their environment. Each of these should be something they actually witness, such as a car driving by, a flying bird, a leaf falling or the movement of a cloud. These are but four of countless examples they could notice and write down. The key to the game is to notice unique examples of change, things that the others likely won't notice.

Once everyone has finished their lists of ten, have one person read his or her list to the others. If anyone noticed the same change, then that one should be crossed out on everyone's page and no points are awarded. Whoever noticed and wrote down something that no one else noticed gets a point. Everyone should take turns reading their lists. The person with the most points is the winner!

Talk about how common change is in our lives and how noticing this can make us think of God who is absolutely unchangeable.

AWE AND WONDER

Can you imagine a God Who acts but is never acted upon? One who never has anything happen to Him or added on to Him? He never changes His mind or His location or His will. And this same God knows everything that can be known in an eternal instantaneous present now. He can't learn or receive anything new.

This is what it means to be immutable, unchangeable. It's so far beyond anything we can ever experience because our world is inherently changeable. We will change between now and the time we finish reading this sentence. We just got older!

How incredible and reassuring it is to know that our great God has none of these limitations. And that this God loves us and wants to share Himself with us. He wants us to rest with Him and know Him in heaven for all of eternity.

PRAYER

My God, I experience change every moment of my life. Help me to better understand that You are immutable and have no need for change, being perfect in every way.

LESSON 11

Is God Outside Time?

Another quality of God that is directly related to His immutability is that He is outside of time, or eternal. This is a difficult concept for us to understand because our very existence is based on time. Time and change are directly related. With time comes change, and with change goes time. As time passes we get older, the seasons change, and we move around from one place to another. Nothing can 'happen' outside of time in our world.

So can you comprehend an existence outside of time? God is perfect and has no need to change locations (He is everywhere). He is never acted upon (He is perfect act) and is outside of time because it doesn't pertain to Him. A God who could be inside of time is a God that changes, and obviously this is contrary to His immutability.

Being outside of time, God does not experience the world successively (going from one thing to the next) but rather all things past, present and future He sees in an eternal now. It's a very difficult concept to comprehend but that's why He is God and we're not!

ST. THOMAS SAYS...

The idea of eternity follows immutability, as the idea of time follows movement, as appears from the preceding article. Hence, as God is supremely immutable, it supremely belongs to Him to be eternal. Nor is He eternal only; but He is His own eternity; whereas, no other being is its own duration, as no other is its own being. Now God is His own uniform being; and hence as He is His own essence, so He is His own eternity.

FUN ACTIVITY FOR CHILDREN

This activity will require at least two players and some device that measures time, such as a watch with a second hand or a stopwatch.

Go into a relatively small room (like an average size bedroom) that has a number of items, such as pictures or furniture or stuffed animals. Everyone participating in the game is allowed three minutes to study the room, paying attention to small details. Next, all but one person should leave the room and the door should be closed. The one person Inside should take a reasonable amount of time (less than five minutes) to make ten changes to the room, such as moving a picture to the other side of the dresser or turning a book upside down. The changes should not be extremely obvious but they also should not be so small that no person would realistically be able to notice them. Once all ten changes have been made and written down, all the other players are allowed to come back into the room. Everyone gets two minutes to review the room and make mental notes of anything that looks to have been changed. When two minutes have passed, the youngest player is given ten seconds to notice one change. If he is right, he gets a point. After he has guessed, the next youngest person is given ten seconds to notice another change. If time runs out, the next person gets to guess. Continue until all ten changes have been found or everyone has run out of guesses. The person with the most points is the winner.

Make sure everyone is able to make a connection between the passing of time for each part of this game and the change that happened during that time. What is the relationship between time and change and how do both relate to God?

OUTSIDE ADVENTURE

It's time to have an outside foot race between as many participants as would like to compete. Figure out a good distance for each participant to run and identify a clear beginning and finish point for the race. It's best if you're able to measure the distance of the run, such as 200 feet or 100 meters or however long you'd like to make the race. You'll also need some device that can time the runners.

The key to this activity is that each of the participants should run individually and each should be timed to see how quickly he or she can complete the race. See if you can make it into a fun competition.

After everyone has run and seen their time, repeat the activity but this time don't keep track of the time. Naturally the participants are going to want to know their times and who won. But this information will not be available.

When finished, talk about the connection between movement, distance covered and time. If you feel ambitious, calculate the speed of the runners by dividing the distance by the time to get their speed.

How does this activity relate to this lesson about God?

AWE AND WONDER

Do you feel a bit of confusion, like your head is spinning when you try to understand the qualities of God that we have considered so far? If so, congratulations! This means you're taking the lessons seriously and you're pondering God's excellence effectively. The truth is most people don't spend enough time wrestling with the truths about God's nature. His nature so far exceeds ours that most don't even try to understand Who He is. If we desire to live with God for eternity, we should begin now thinking about Him and searching for Him every day. Is there any better way we could spend our time?

We must realize, however, that we will never fully comprehend God, not even in heaven. Because if we fully comprehended Him, we would be Him! But with study, reflection and a lot of prayer (and the outpouring of His Grace), we can come to know Him as best our limited minds are able. So rather than be frustrated with how difficult it is to understand God, let's rejoice that we worship a God that is so awesome, so far above us. It would be more alarming if God was totally understandable to our little minds. What would this say about God? Don't we prefer Him to be a great mystery?

PRAYER

My God, I desire to know You and live with You forever. I know I am limited in my ability to comprehend You, but please reveal to me as much about Yourself as you desire for me to know, and grant me the wisdom to seek You always with great ardor and zeal.

LESSON 12

Can We Know God?

Now that we've learned a lot about our awesome God Who surpasses us in many ways, you might be wondering whether it's even possible that we can come to know Him in a personal way.

Any intellectual creature (such as a human being) can come to know other things in their essences, including God Himself. So if God created us with a nature that is capable of knowing Him, then we must trust that God will certainly provide a way for us to accomplish this goal! And it's important to know this fact about God... He is knowable to intellectual creatures. We can come to know God! In fact, it is for this reason that we were created, and this also explains why everyone has a longing (desire) in their hearts to know God. Take a moment to recall everything we've learned about God, from His utter simplicity to His perfection and Goodness. God wants us to know Him and has provided us with a nature that allows us to do it!

ST. THOMAS SAYS...

Since everything is knowable according as it is actual, God, Who is pure act without any admixture of potentiality, is in Himself supremely knowable. But what is supremely knowable in itself, may not be knowable to a particular intellect, on account of the excess of the intelligible object above the intellect...The ultimate beatitude of man consists in the use of his highest function, which is the operation of his intellect; if we suppose that the created intellect could never see God, it would either never attain to beatitude, or its beatitude would consist in something else beside God; which is opposed to faith.... Also, there resides in every man a natural desire to know the cause of any effect which he sees; and thence arises wonder in men. But if the intellect of the rational creature could not reach so far as to the first cause of things, the natural desire would remain void.

FUN ACTIVITY FOR CHILDREN

Let's play a game where we hide a surprise and then make clues for our sibling or friend to try to find it. Either buy a surprise (like a candy bar or small toy) or use one of your own toys as the prize. Hide it somewhere in your house. Then on four pieces of paper write clues to help your friend or sibling find it. For example, on a first piece of paper you might write 'look under my pillow.' Then place another piece of paper under your pillow that says 'look in the refrigerator' for the next clue. Let the final clue lead the person to where you have hidden the surprise.

Was the game fun? Did your friend or sibling find the surprise? Why was he or she able to find it? It's because you developed a game that allowed them to use their particular qualities (ability to read, understand, etc.) to follow the instructions, right?

Now discuss the answers to these questions:

1. What if the prize at the end didn't exist? What effect would that have had on the game?

2. What if your clues had not effectively led your friend or sibling to the end prize? How would that have impacted the game?

Try to make the connection between this simple game and the objective of this lesson, namely, how we are able to come to know God (through the many clues about Him that surround us every day).

OUTSIDE ADVENTURE

This activity will hopefully be fun while also being a bit frustrating. But it's all designed to make a point related to the lesson.

Do one or all of the following activities: Slice up some watermelon cubes and put them on a paper plate on a table outside. Make as many plates as there are participants. Have everyone race to see how quickly they can finish the watermelon on their plates with one catch... they can't use their hands!

You could also make a few dozen water balloons and

line up the participants about 10-15 feet away from the bucket with the balloons. Next, take turns throwing a single balloon at each participant, one at a time, and ask them to try to catch the balloon, but again without using their hands!

See who can figure out how these frustrating (and hopefully fun) activities are related to this lesson about coming to know God. And see if you can think of other such activities that highlight the same point.

AWE AND WONDER

You've likely heard of a pair of brothers from America named Orville and Wilbur Wright. They've been credited with Inventing, building and flying the world's first airplane. The successful, historic flight happened near Kitty Hawk, North Carolina on December 17, 1903. Their accomplishment came after many years of hard work, research and trials. Previous to getting involved in aviation, the brothers had worked on printing presses, in a bicycle shop, on motors and other machinery. They knew their success depended on building a plane that had the right wings, propellers, engine, equilibrium and axis control, so that the pilot could control the airplane in flight.

You might wonder what the Wright Brothers have to do with this particular lesson about our ability to know God. Well, the Wright Brothers were focused on a very specific goal and purpose: to create a plane that could be successfully controlled and flown by a pilot. You and I were created by God with a very specific purpose and end in mind. Our purpose is to know God and our purpose is to be united with Him forever in heaven. Our success or failure will depend on whether we fulfill our purpose.

PRAYER

My God, thank You for creating me as an intelligent being capable of knowing You, desiring You and living with You forever in heaven.

LESSON 13

How Can I Best Know God?

In John 14:2, Jesus says that in His house there are many rooms. This has been interpreted to mean that there are distinct 'levels' in the afterlife. In this lesson we will learn that some people in heaven will possess a greater glory and will therefore 'see' or know God better than others. Remember in the last lesson that with God's help we can come to know Him. In heaven we will know Him in a much better way than now and some will know better than others.

You might wonder what one person does in order to reach the highest degree of heaven possible, and why others do not reach so high a level of glory. St. Thomas teaches that in heaven God will not change from one person to the next. He will be the same for everyone.

What does change, however, is our capacity to see and know Him, which is determined according to God's Grace and our own disposition or attitude toward God. Some will have what St. Thomas calls a greater 'light of glory' than others.

So what makes the difference? St. Thomas teaches that the person with greater charity, or love of God, will naturally desire Him more, and this person will see Him more clearly than others.

ST. THOMAS SAYS...

Of those who see the essence of God, one sees Him more perfectly than another. This, indeed, does not take place as if one had a more perfect similitude of God than another, since that vision will not spring from any similitude; but it will take place because one intellect will have a greater power or faculty to see God than another. The faculty of seeing God, however, does not belong to the created intellect naturally, but is given to it by the light of glory...

Hence the intellect which has more of the light of glory will see God the more perfectly; and he will have a fuller participation of the light of glory who has more charity; because where there is the greater charity, there is the more desire; and desire in a certain degree makes the one desiring apt and prepared to receive the object desired.

FUN ACTIVITY FOR CHILDREN

Each of the children should make their own personal 'dream book' of five of their favorite things to do or have. The dream book can be made any way the child chooses, but what's important is that each of the five things should be able to be presented as a 'ticket' to their parents at an appropriate time.

Examples of things in the 'dream book' could be going out to dinner at a restaurant of their choice, going out for an ice cream cone, staying up thirty minutes late one night, being served breakfast In bed on a Saturday morning, or not having to clean their room for a day. These are just examples. Each child should easily be able to come up with his or her own list of 'dream things' for their tickets.

At appropriate times when it's possible to do the thing indicated on the child's ticket, he or she can present a ticket to the parents for permission to play a game for a chance to win the activity or treat. Next, the child must win two out of three games of Paper, Scissors, Rock against one of his or her parents. If they win, they get whatever was on the particular ticket that was presented to the parents. If they lose, they don't get the prize and must wait at least a day until they can try again.

The key to this activity is for the child to pay attention to the desire he or she has for the things written on their 'dream book' tickets, especially at the time when he or she is playing the game. How does this game relate to our desire for God, and how much control do we have for the intensity of that desire?

OUTSIDE ADVENTURE

Once outside have each person write down the first five things that he or she sees that are moving, such as a dragonfly, butterfly, a dog or cat, or even a car or a person running down the street. Beside each of the five action items, take a guess at what each of these creatures or things 'desires.' See if you can put yourself in their place and figure out why each is moving, to where they are likely going, and how their movement is an Indication of a particular desire that each has. Ask yourself whether each would be moving if there was no desire to get somewhere or do something. Try to think 'outside the box' and apply desire (or sometimes called appetite) to many of the things you see each day.

Recall previous lessons about 'instinct' and also about the pursuit of an end for all individual creatures and the world as a whole. Talk about how each of these movements is related to these topics.

AWE AND WONDER

Can we really control how much we desire God? In one way yes, and in another way no. Just as we can't force ourselves to like someone whom we don't care for, or desire a particular kind of food that we simply don't like, we also can't force ourselves to desire or love God as we should. But if you read this lesson and have a desire to love God more because you want to know Him and experience the greatest 'light of glory' in heaven, then God's grace is already working in your soul and you are on your way to a greater desire and love of God. And when the time comes that you are struggling to desire Him as you wish, you always have recourse to prayer. The very desire to desire is a movement of God's grace and should be seen as a gift which one should open with joy! And if we respond to this grace by asking for an even greater desire to know and love God more, don't you think God will honor such a sincere prayer?

PRAYER

My God, I want to desire You more than I do now. Please give me the grace to desire You more so that I can know and experience You with the greatest 'light of glory' as You desire for me.

LESSON 14

Does God Have A Favorite Name?

So far we've dedicated most of the first thirteen lessons to getting to know this incredible God with Whom we hope to spend eternity—praising, knowing and loving Him as much as possible through the light of glory, which He will grant us according to our charity and desire for Him. We've also learned a lot about God's nature. He is simple, perfect, all-knowing, eternal, unchangeable and supremely knowable and the Creator of all that is good.

Now that we know a lot about Him, you likely have a desire to know how to best address Him. In other words, does He have a favorite name for Himself, one that truly describes Who He is and What He is and does? Keep in mind that a wonderful man from the Old Testament named Moses once asked God this very question, namely, what are we to call Him? And God gave Moses the answer: His name is 'I Am Who Am' or 'He Who Is' or more simply 'I am.' This seems like a strange name, doesn't it? But it's the perfect name for God because it best describes Who He is and most perfectly describes His nature. But how so? It's because this name 'I am' describes God in His simplicity, His life in the eternal now and His unique unchangeableness, the qualities of God that we learned about in previous lessons. And remember, God Is existence itself.

ST. THOMAS SAYS...

This name HE WHO IS is most properly applied to God, for three reasons:

First, It does not signify form, but simply existence itself. Hence, since the existence of God is His essence itself.

Secondly, on account of its universality. Now our intellect cannot know the essence of God itself in this life, as it is in itself, but whatever mode it applies in determining what it understands about God, it falls short of the mode of what God is in Himself. Therefore, the less determinate the names are, and the more universal and absolute they are, the more properly they are applied to God.

Thirdly…. because… it signifies present existence; and this above all properly applies to God, whose existence knows not past or future.

FUN ACTIVITY FOR CHILDREN

With this activity we're going to participate in an indoor scavenger hunt. Divide the participants into two groups. Each group should come up with five things that can be found in the home for the other team to find. The trick, however, is that the proper name of the items can't be used in the description. Write down each of the five things on a piece of paper. So rather than writing 'scissors' you might write 'double bladed cutting tool' and instead of a 'book' you could write 'multi-page paper packet for reading purposes.'

The key here is to learn to describe things according to what they are and for what is their purpose rather than just by the name we've come to associate with them.

Once each team has written down their five descriptions, trade pieces of paper and see which team can find the other team's five items first.

Be sure to discuss how this lesson relates to God's name and nature as explained in the introductory paragraph.

OUTSIDE ADVENTURE

Now that you've done this fun scavenger hunt activity indoors, let's go outside and play a similar but different game in the midst of God's creation.

Select one person to go first. This person should identify some aspect of nature, such as a cloud or a squirrel or the green grass and then try to describe the thing to the others without using the actual name of the word. So for grass, one might say 'it's green, comes up in blades out of the ground and we mow it.' When someone correctly guesses, it becomes his or her turn to begin describing something that is in sight. It's important that the thing that is described be in view of everyone who is present for the game.

Hopefully this game will help everyone realize that the

words we use, the names we give to things, are packed with meaning. When we hear a word such as 'bird,' our minds understand a lot about a bird beyond just the name. We think of flight, of feathers, perhaps a beak and other parts of the bird's nature. The name is an abbreviation of sorts for the creature's essence and nature.

How does this relate to God and His favorite name?

AWE AND WONDER

Contemplate these words, 'He Who Is' and 'I Am' for a while, trying to really unpack the meaning behind the name. Think of the beauty of the words in reflecting God's utter simplicity. It's not past tense or future tense but present tense, because God exists in the eternal now. God is existence. Let that sink in. God's essence (What He is) and His existence (That He is) are the same thing. Can you even get your mind around this idea of God as being Being itself? He is everywhere and all things and perfections pre-exist in Him. Consider a time when you were excited to find out someone's name because you found them so intriguing. Why did you want to know their name so badly? What is so important about a name? Why do you think it was important for God to tell us His name?

PRAYER

My God, help me to understand You as 'He Who Is' and 'I Am.' Enlighten me to best understand this name as best describing Your essence and nature.

LESSON 15

Does God Know Everything?

Up until now our reflection and study of God has focused primarily on what He doesn't have (doesn't change, doesn't move, doesn't have a body, doesn't get acted upon or moved) and what He is not (not caused, not inside time), rather than on what God does have and is. Now let's consider an extremely important part of St. Thomas' philosophy: God's knowledge.

Have you ever thought about what it means to know something? We know our friends and family members. We know facts and dates and phone numbers and objects like chairs and clocks, and it's important to be reminded that St. Thomas says our ultimate happiness will be 'to know God' perfectly one day In heaven. But what exactly is knowledge and what does God know? To know is to understand a thing, and understanding can only be carried out by a rational creature. Dogs and bunnies and flies do not understand and therefore cannot come to know things in their essences as we do. But God knows everything perfectly.

In fact, God knows everything, past, present, future. Everything without exception. And as we learn in this lesson, God's knowledge is the cause of things. Things are because He knows. That's right—because God knows us, we exist. And as you'll see below, God's knowledge is joined by His will (intellectual desire), and this is what holds everything in existence.

ST. THOMAS SAYS...

The knowledge of God is the cause of things. For the knowledge of God is to all creatures what the knowledge of the 'artist' is to things made by his art. Now the knowledge of the artificer is the cause of the things made by his art from the fact that the artificer works by his intellect. Hence the form of the intellect must be the principle of action.... Now it is clear that God causes things by His intellect, since His being is His act of understanding; and hence His knowledge must be the cause of things, insofar as His will is joined to it.

FUN ACTIVITY FOR CHILDREN

This activity may require a trip to the hobby or arts and crafts store for some very simple and Inexpensive supplies. The items suggested for this activity can easily be substituted with something you already have in the home as long as the purpose of the lesson is not lost.

Give each child participant twenty ice pop sticks and some simple glue. Send each child to a different place in the home and allow them 10-15 minutes to create with these simple supplies whatever they'd like to make and wherever their creativity takes them. Try to not provide any suggestions so that what they create comes directly from their own imagination as a reflection of their unique personality and gifts.

When the time is up, ask all the children to come back

together and let them explain, one at a time, what they created with the ice pop sticks and glue. It's very likely that each of their creations will be completely unique.

Talk about the connection between this simple activity and the purpose of this lesson. Didn't these creations come from a concept in their minds, from their own intelligence? And isn't each of their creations a reflection of themselves?

OUTSIDE ADVENTURE

Go outside to a place where you can see a lot of different examples of God's beauty of creation. Appoint someone to be the timekeeper and have another person be the scribe. At least one additional person should participate in the activity. When the timekeeper says 'go,' each participant should visually lock into something in nature, such as a tree or a rock or a shrub, anything in view. Once they decide what to look at, they should say out loud to the scribe what they're looking at and he or she will write it down. During this time the participants should focus on the features of the object, paying close attention to the object. After twenty seconds the timekeeper will say 'switch' and each participant should visually lock in to something else In view. Do this a total of ten times at twenty second intervals as announced by the timekeeper. So at the end of the tenth round the scribe should have ten things listed on the paper for each participant.

Next, the scribe should ask each participant to recall

how many of the objects he or she remembers from their list. See who can remember the most. This is a good activity highlighting the way our minds work, going from one thing to the next, but without knowing them all at the same time. In light of this lesson, how does this compare to God's knowledge?

AWE AND WONDER

Sometimes it's hard to imagine that God can care about us as individuals, when at the same time He loves billions of other people who are living on the earth (not to mention those who previously lived or will live in the future). Can God really care about each of us as individual beings on this huge earth filled with so many other humans as well as countless other creatures?

Consider that according to the Population Census Bureau, there are currently about seven and a half billion (7,500,000,000) people living on the earth. The bureau estimates that approximately 107 billion people (107,000,000,000) are either living or have lived at some time. And science has proved that each one of these individual persons is absolutely unique from the moment of his or her conception/fertilization. Who could possibly accomplish this other than a loving, all knowing God who knows and wills each of us into existence?

PRAYER

Lord, help me to be aware that because of Your knowledge of me, I exist at this moment. Please give me the grace to always be thankful for the gift of my life and the lives of all creatures in the world.

LESSON 16

What Are Ideas?

Have you ever had a great idea or told someone you had no idea what they're talking about? I'm sure you have. But what are ideas and what have they to do with God?

The key to understanding 'ideas' in this lesson is training ourselves to think abstractly—in other words, to think about things outside of the physical universe that our senses can perceive. It's the difference between thinking of a pizza abstractly, as a concept in our minds, and actually experiencing an individual pizza with the great smell and taste and touch! One is tangible and experienced by our senses while the other is intangible, conceptual and outside the grasp of our senses.

In this lesson we learn that the 'idea' of all things exists in the mind of God. We will also consider what is referred to as the essence of a thing in the abstract, which is often described in philosophy as 'treeness' or 'dogness' or 'chairness' when referring to the essence of a tree, a dog or a chair. This is the abstract 'idea' or the concept of the tree or the dog or the chair, rather than the physical, tangible individual object itself. Only creatures with reason and intelligence can conceive of 'ideas.'

ST. THOMAS SAYS...

It is necessary to suppose ideas in the divine mind. For the Greek word {Idea} is in Latin "forma." Hence, by ideas are understood the forms of things, existing apart from the things themselves. Now the form of anything existing apart from the thing itself can be for one of two ends: either to be the type of that of which it is called the form, or to be the principle of the knowledge of that thing, inasmuch as the forms of things knowable are said to be in him who knows them.

FUN ACTIVITY FOR CHILDREN

Choose one person who is going to lead the activity and all of the others will participate. It's important to have at least three total participants. Each of the participants should have some sort of pen or marker and a piece of paper. The leader chooses some noun, such as 'dog' or 'tree' or 'person,' anything that is generic and not specific. So for example, they can't say the name of a specific person such as 'Uncle Charlie' or the name of a famous celebrity like 'Thomas Jefferson' or something of that sort. Once the leader decides on the word, they should say the single word out loud without any other details.

Next, each of the participants, set apart and out of view from each other, should draw a picture of the word that was spoken. Make sure each person draws only one thing, not a variety of things. So if it's 'dog,' everyone on their own draws a single dog.

Once everyone is finished, have everyone come together and compare their drawings. Notice how despite everyone drawing the same word that was spoken, each picture looks different and unique.

See if this can lead to a discussion of the difference from the abstract and the specific in regard to how our minds come to know things.

OUTSIDE ADVENTURE

Once outside, we're going to see how our minds differentiate between the abstract and the specific just about every moment of every day. Have everyone except one person close their eyes while the leader finds something in nature that they find Intriguing. Perhaps they see a grasshopper or a beautiful flower or a butterfly traveling across the yard. Once the leader has identified their object, they should say out loud a generic description of what they see, such as 'grasshopper' or 'flower.'

Next, those that have closed their eyes should begin asking questions about what the object looks like, such as, regarding the grasshopper, 'is it big or small?' or 'is it green?' The leader should answer all the questions until the participants think they have a good idea in their mind of how it looks.

Once finished with the questions, the participants can

open their eyes and view the object that the leader saw. Most likely they will realize that even with all the clues and answers to their questions, their 'Idea' of what the object looks like falls short of reality.

Does this help you to understand the concept of 'ideas' as it relates to this lesson?

AWE AND WONDER

When you consider an 'idea' of something you've experienced in your life, you should thank God that you are able to do this. That's because the 'thinking' or conceiving of ideas is only possible for rational, intellectual creatures. Irrational animals (like bears and squirrels and ladybugs) are not able to understand ideas. It's not in their nature to do so. This is reserved only for intelligent creatures like us and the angels (and our uncreated God). But God does not come to know ideas like we do. Rather, the ideas of all things exist in His mind already in a single 'glance' or moment, outside of time. It's our task to come to know the ideas of things as are first known by God. So the next time you say 'I have an idea,' take notice of the privilege of being able to say this. Dogs and cats and worms don't have 'ideas.' They only experience things with their senses but not with an intellect. Knowing ideas is part of what makes us like God. It's no small thing!

PRAYER

My God, thank You for creating me as an intelligent creature made to Your image and likeness, capable of knowing the ideas of all things. Please help me use my intellect and will for Your greater glory and honor.

LESSON 17

What Does God Want?

Most of us spend a lot of time thinking about what we want, both from others and from God. You could likely make a list right now of ten things you desire at this moment. But have you ever stopped to consider what God wants? Or perhaps you've wondered whether God wants anything since He's perfect in every way. What could He possibly want that He doesn't already have? We've already learned that God is existence itself so He contains in Himself the perfection of all things! What else could He desire?

St. Thomas says that all intellectual creatures have will, that is, they have what can be called 'intellectual desire.' But what does God desire? God desires to communicate His goodness, His beauty and His Truth, His very self to the rest of creation. We know that whatever exists right now, including you and me, exist because God wants us to exist. He also wants us to experience everything that He possesses, which is all that is good, beautiful and true. Isn't this an exciting truth to contemplate?

ST. THOMAS SAYS...

It pertains....to the nature of the will to communicate as far as possible to others the good possessed; and especially does this pertain to the divine will, from which all perfection is derived in some kind of likeness. Hence, if natural things, insofar as they are perfect, communicate their good to others, much more does it appertain to the divine will to communicate by likeness its own good to others as much as possible. Thus then, He wills both Himself to be, and other things to be; but Himself as the end, and other things as ordained to that end; inasmuch as it befits the divine goodness that other things should be partakers therein.

FUN ACTIVITY FOR CHILDREN

With your mom and/or dad's permission and help, make a few small gifts that can be given to your neighbors or friends. For example, bake a dozen or two chocolate chip cookies and put them on a paper plate and wrap them with some plastic wrap. Or simply buy some flowers and make a few small bouquets that can be brought over to the neighbors' homes. You can likely think of other similar ideas depending on your talent and what your neighbors would like to receive. The key is that the gifts should be nice and require a little creativity and sacrifice on your part in the preparation. Next, go to the home of some of your neighbors or friends, knock on their door and give them the gift, explaining that you're doing it because you value their friendship and wanted to bless them with a gift that they would enjoy. Once you've done this, answer the following questions…

1. How did your neighbors or friends respond to the gift?

2. How did you feel giving the gifts to your neighbors?

3. How do you think this will impact your relationship with your neighbors?

4. How do you think this activity relates to this lesson?

OUTSIDE ADVENTURE

In this adventure, we want to take notice of the many ways God's creatures bless us and make our lives better. We want to pay attention to the 'big picture' of how God has provided for us blessings through the created world, and the gifts that some of these creatures provide for us. Use your Imagination and think of creatures you can visit that God has used to bless you. Here are a few examples and perhaps you can think of others.

- Maybe there are cows, chickens, pigs or other farm animals not too far from your home. These animals bless us with food and drinks that most of us enjoy every day, not to mention items of clothing such as leather jackets and shoes.

- Find some bees nearby and talk about the delicious honey that these creatures provide.

- Are there birds, crickets or cicadas nearby that add beautiful sounds to our day?

- Do the clouds provide the rainwater that keeps our grass green and lakes filled up?

Now it's up to you to go out and find some of these creatures or think of some others on your own. Be sure when you see them, to make the connection between their particular 'gifts' to us and our very generous God!

AWE AND WONDER

Isn't it refreshing to know that God's desire is for us to be happy and that His desire is to communicate His Goodness to us? Properly understood, this should give us tremendous relief and comfort, because it means that He is completely in control and He has created a world that is designed to provide for all of our needs. Remember in a previous lesson how we learned that it would be odd for us to have an intellect that desires God without there being a God Whom we can know? In the same way it would seem very odd to have a nature that desires certain foods (like beef and pork, strawberries and apples) and drinks (like milk) without God providing a way for us to satisfy those desires. By looking at the way God has designed our world, it is easy to see that He's got everything figured out, and He's done everything necessary to ensure we are able to be healthy and happy.

Perhaps as a child you had that certainty that

everything was going to be just fine because you had absolute trust in your parents. This is exactly the kind of trust we should have in God. We should imagine God whispering in our ear every day, 'Everything will be fine. I am in control. My will is always fulfilled and I want the best for you. Do not worry.' Can we bring ourselves to that level of trust in God?

PRAYER

My God, please help me to understand that Your will is perfect and that you love me and desire the best for me. Please give me the grace to trust You regardless of the circumstances in my life.

LESSON 18

Does God Love Some Creatures More Than Others?

Does God love your dog or cat as much as He loves you? In one way, God loves all His creatures equally because He created them all as reflections of His own Goodness. But in another way, it can be proved that God loves you more than He loves your dog or your cat or the beautiful rosebush out in your back garden, (even though it probably smells better than you). While some may be surprised by this, most of us naturally assume this to be true. But the dog and cat and rosebush can't sin or offend God and we can, right? So why does God love us more than these other creatures?

Most likely you aren't able to explain exactly why this is the case, other than to say that you have a greater dignity than these animals, and you are made to God's image and likeness. While these are both true, let's dig a little deeper. How can we know that He loves some creatures more than others? Well, it's quite simple. He loves that creature more for whom He plans a greater good. What is the greatest good possible for a grub worm, a bird, a dog or a human being? We'll explore this question more in the fun activity below.

ST. THOMAS SAYS...

Since to love a thing is to will it good, in a two-fold way anything may be loved more, or less. In one way on the part of the act of the will itself, which is more or less intense. In this way, God does not love some things more than others, because He loves all things by an act of the will that is one, simple, and always the same. In another way, on the part of the good itself that a person wills for the beloved. In this way, we are said to love that one more than another, for whom we will a greater good, though our will is not more intense. In this way we must need to say that God loves some things more than others. For since God's love is the cause of goodness in things, no one thing would be better than another, if God did not will greater good for one than for another.

FUN ACTIVITY FOR CHILDREN

This is going to be a different kind of activity that requires each child to write a short story on a given topic. First, write the following words on small pieces of paper: Rock, Butterfly, Cat, Dog and Human Being. Place the five pieces of paper in a hat or can, and have each child draw from the hat one of the pieces of paper.

Next, each child should look at the name of the creature they've picked and write a story, being as creative as possible, of the 'dream day' of this particular creature. The only stipulation is that it must be realistic. For example, he or she can't have the butterfly driving a car or the dog reading a book or flying a rocket to the moon. The story must speak of a perfect and realistic day in regard to the particular nature of the creature they've chosen.

Feel free to put limitations on the length of the story, of the time each child can take to write his or her story. Hopefully you'll have five participants but if not, ask some to write more than one story. It's important that all five creatures' stories be told.

Once everyone is finished, have each child read his or her story out loud. Have some fun comparing the 'perfect day' of each of these creatures as described in the stories and discuss how it relates to this lesson.

OUTSIDE ADVENTURE

Let's take a trip to the zoo! When possible, go to your local zoo and bring along a pen and a journal or something on which to take notes during the visit.

While observing the various animals, write down as many of their names as possible, and beside each write down what you think would be the best part of being that kind of animal. For example, what would be most exciting about being a giraffe or an elephant or a snake? Be as descriptive as possible, but be sure to take note of at least about twenty different animals during your visit.

When you're finished or on the way home, discuss the animals you saw and compare what each child considered to be the best feature of that animal and what would be fun about being that kind of creature.

Finally, ask this question to the children. If you were able, would you permanently trade places with any of the animals you saw at the zoo? Why or why not?

AWE AND WONDER

This lesson might tempt us to become puffed up with pride, realizing that among all of God's creatures we are among the most loved, and have been promised the opportunity to receive the greatest reward, perfect knowledge of God in heaven. But what should be the proper response to learning that we are made to God's image and likeness and are His beloved sons and daughters? Realizing we have received God's favor should fill us with sincere humility and gratitude. Recall how in the Gospel Jesus says, "Let the children come to me, and do not prevent them; for the kingdom of heaven belongs to such as these." Jesus is saying that there is something about a child we should all imitate.

One saint who perfected child-like faith is the 19th century French Carmelite St. Therese of Lisieux, best known for her autobiography called *The Story of a Soul*, in which she explains a profound spirituality known as 'the little way of child-like faith.' In 1997 St. Therese was declared a Universal Doctor of the Church by Pope John Paul II. The Holy Father recognized that during her brief life, St. Therese modeled a child-like trust in her heavenly Father. This trust was made possible by an attitude of complete abandonment and dependence on God the Father. St. Therese took to heart what St. Paul wrote in his second letter to the Corinthians, 'When I am weak then I am strong.'

PRAYER

Dear God, thank You for creating me as a human being, made to Your image and likeness. I did nothing to deserve such a privilege. Please never let me squander the gift and responsibility that I've received.

LESSON 19

What Is Providence?

To say that God has providence over all things simply means that He's in total control of the world and all His creatures. And it means that God is directing all things to their proper end. Remember in a previous lesson that one of the proofs of God's existence is that irrational animals always act toward the end which is best suited to their nature. They naturally do what is best for their own survival and for the survival of their species. For example, ducks fly south in the winter, not because they decide to do it, but because God 'decided' for them to do it, because it's best for them and their offspring and the whole world.

This is very important for us to understand, because it relates to the purpose of all things in the world and how all things work together for the good of the whole. Why do things behave the way they do and who is in charge of it all? A good understanding of this principle will fundamentally change the way we see the world and live our lives.

Recall that we too are being directed to our final end (heaven), but God has also blessed all rational creatures (such as you and I) with free will. This makes us more complicated than the irrational animals because we can fail in our purpose and end, whereas they cannot fail. This is why it's so important to understand God's will and make sure that our wills conform to it, because His will is perfect and ours are not always so.

96

ST. THOMAS SAYS...

All things are subject to divine providence, not only in general, but even in their own individual selves...For since every agent acts for an end, the ordering of effects towards that end extends as far as the causality of the first agent extends...Hence all things that exist in whatsoever manner are necessarily directed by God towards some end.

FUN ACTIVITY FOR CHILDREN

Find a set of dominoes if you have them and if not, set up some series of objects that will act the same as dominos (when one is pushed it pushes the next down and then the next, etc.) If more than one child is playing, give them each the same number of dominos and have them compete to see who can set up their dominos, knock the first and have them all fall over one by one.

Afterwards, have a discussion about the actions of all the individual dominos (or objects) in the series. Did the person who pushed the first domino cause all of them to fall or just the first? And did each domino have any say about whether it was going to fall and knock down the next one or did it just happen? And did the person who knocked the first domino know what was going to happen to all of them? How does this scenario relate to God's providence? And how might the scenario have been different had one of the dominos had free will?

If this demonstration provokes a fun and lively discussion of God's providence in the world and His impact on creatures, great!

OUTSIDE ADVENTURE

Let's go outside with a pad of paper and pen and find the nearest tree. Study the tree for a few minutes and write down what you think are its most fascinating features. Is it tall or short? Note the colors of the leaves and bark? What else do you notice about the tree that perhaps you've never considered before?

Next, draw on your paper a diagram or artistic representation of the process called photosynthesis, a word which literally means 'light' and 'to put together.' Consider how this tree is able to 'breathe in' carbon dioxide, absorb light from the sun and 'drink' water with its elaborate root system in the ground. The light, water and carbon dioxide are then 'put together' by the tree to create sugar and oxygen.

Write this formula for photosynthesis below your picture or diagram:

light + water + carbon dioxide = sugar + oxygen.

Why is this important? Well, we as humans need oxygen in order to live. We need this tree and other trees and plants to make the oxygen that is necessary for our survival. Where does the tree get the carbon dioxide it needs? From us because we exhale the carbon dioxide necessary for the process of photosynthesis. The tree also needs food but since it can't move it must have a way to make its own. The tree's food is the sugar that it makes through the process of photosynthesis.

Can you see how this simple tree and others like it provide a perfect example to help explain and understand God's providence in the world? Has this changed the way you see the tree?

AWE AND WONDER

Take a moment to ponder the last sentence in the quote from St. Thomas Aquinas above, 'Hence all things that exist in whatsoever manner are necessarily directed by God towards some end.' Notice the very specific wording of the quote. 'All things' means just that. Every single thing created by God, which consists of animals, plants, planets, humans and angels, to name but a few. Then he says that all these things are 'necessarily directed by God to some end.' How often do we hear this when speaking about the creatures in the world, that all things are directed by God to their end in some way? The world is so amazingly organized that it only makes sense that there is a great Mind, a super Intellect and Will that is directing everything to a grand final end.

The fifth proof for the existence of God explains that all these wonderful creatures exist only possibly, which means at one time they did not exist and therefore it's certainly possible that they could possibly have never existed. They're only possible and not necessary. But since all creatures have this quality in common, it also true that at one time none of these creatures could have existed. But we know that they do in fact exist, and this means that there must be 'Something' in existence that is not only possible but necessary, and this necessary Being is God.

PRAYER

My Lord, thank You for bringing order to the world through Your providence. And thank You for the world You have created and for giving me the freedom to love You and others and to be obedient to Your perfect will.

LESSON 20

Are We God's Robots?

This question may sound ridiculous because you know you're very different from a robot. You know that you have a lot of control over your daily actions and decisions. But how do we find a solution to what may seem as a conflict between God's providence over all creation and our ability to choose our own actions?

The key here is a further review of that very important word in relation to St. Thomas' philosophy and theology, nature. Nature not only concerns what things are—as humans or dogs or salamanders or angels— but also the purpose and end of each of these creatures. Remember, we've learned that God equips every creature with a nature that is suitable to achieving its proper end. But not all creatures have been blessed with the nature that allows them to know God, as has already been discussed. Some creatures are somewhat robotic in that they have no free will or ultimate control over their actions. But since our nature includes free will, we are far from being pre-programmed robots. God has given us a nature that can choose to love Him or not love Him, obey or not obey Him, and live with Him forever or live apart from Him. And He does this without limiting His providence over all of creation or causing His perfect will to be changed or altered.

ST. THOMAS SAYS...

Divine providence imposes necessity upon some things; not upon all…. For to providence it belongs to order things towards an end. Now after the divine goodness, which is an extrinsic end to all things, the principal good in things themselves is the perfection of the universe; which would not be, were not all grades of being found in things. Whence it pertains to divine providence to produce every grade of being. And thus it has prepared for some things necessary causes, so that they happen of necessity; for others contingent causes, that they may happen by contingency, according to the nature of their proximate causes.

FUN ACTIVITY FOR CHILDREN

This activity will require at least two participants and if more than two, it should be done in pairs.

This is called the 'robot game.' With each pair of children, decide who will first act as the robot and who will control the robot. Explain that for ten minutes the 'robot' will be controlled by the other child. This means that they don't move, speak or do anything unless they are instructed to do so. So if the first child says, 'Go make my bed' or 'get me a glass of water' the robot must do what it has been commanded to do. The robot only says what it's told to say. The 'robot' can't move or do anything without being told to do it. It's important that the 'robot' understands that during this activity it has no free will and is being totally controlled by the other child. Once ten minutes has passed, have them trade roles and do the activity for another ten minutes.

After they're finished, have them discuss the following questions:

1. Did you enjoy more being the robot or the one controlling the robot?

2. Would you like your friend to be a robot that does whatever you tell them to do, or would you rather have your friend as he or she is in real life?

3. Do you think God controls you as If you're a robot or not?

OUTSIDE ADVENTURE

Go out to where you have some room and play a fun game of 'Simon Says' and see how this relates to this lesson.

Either an adult or one of the children calls out Instructions to the whole group, such as 'Simon says jump once' or 'Simon says do five jumping jacks' of something similar. The catch is that if an instruction Is called out without the preface 'Simon says' then the participants are not to do what they've been asked to do. For example, if the leader says 'Do five pushups!' then no one should react because there was no 'Simon says' at the beginning. When someone makes a mistake they must leave the game. When you're down to just one player, that's the winner of the game!

Next, have everyone observe some of God's creatures in the natural world, such as the birds flying overhead, or the beautiful butterfly or bumblebee or cat that you can see. Discuss whether their motions are 'robotic' in the sense that someone is telling them what to do or playing a big game of 'Simon says' like they just played. Or do the creatures have a certain 'free will' to do as they choose. How does this reflection change the way we see the natural world?

AWE AND WONDER

Wouldn't it have been much easier if God had created us as robots who obeyed His every command, rather than leaving us free to choose for or against Him? Wouldn't this solve the problem of all the evil in the world? Couldn't God have created a world where sin and evil and rebellion were not possible? If God is perfect and knows what is absolutely right for us, why would He take such a big chance by allowing us to choose either for or against Him? But God did decide to give us the ability to decide whether to obey or disobey Him.

Why do you think God gave us such an incredible freedom? Could we have loved God without free will? Can a fox or beaver or porcupine love God? Ponder the incredible responsibility we have in light of this gift from God. How should we respond to a God who gives us such freedom and responsibility?

PRAYER

My God, You have given me freedom to love You or not love You, to obey You or not obey You, and to choose to live with You or apart from You forever. Please give me the grace to respond to You with obedience and love.

LESSON 21

What is Beatitude?

What would make you perfectly happy? If you asked ten people this question, you'd likely get ten different answers. But what if there was a word that could describe what will make every single person happy without exception? Well, there is such a word—Beatitude, which is another word for perfect happiness. And the fascinating thing about happiness is that, despite the vast differences in each of the billions of people who have lived or are living now or will live in the future, we all share one thing in common. Everyone wants to be happy.

If we all share this one quality in common, it would make sense to figure out what exactly this happiness is that we all desire and how we can achieve it. This is where our study of Christian philosophy and theology comes together nicely. We've already learned that all perfections in the natural world pre-exist in God. So if you bundled up all the perfections and all the things that we think make us happy, the end result would be...God! And He'd still be more!

Now we can begin to understand that this wonderful God, this perfect and all-powerful Being, whom we have come to know through these lessons, is our perfect happiness. Knowing Him, loving Him, and being with Him is our final end and purpose. Our happiness is God. God is beatitude! God is drawing us to Himself every moment of every day, surrounding us with beauty and goodness and many things that make us happy now, so that we will have a foretaste of the perfect happiness that awaits us in Heaven.

ST. THOMAS SAYS...

Beatitude belongs to God in a very special manner. For nothing else is understood to be meant by the term beatitude than the perfect good of an intellectual nature; which is capable of knowing that it has a sufficiency of the good which it possesses, to which it is competent that good or ill may befall, and which can control its own actions. All of these things belong in a most excellent manner to God, namely, to be perfect, and to possess intelligence. Whence beatitude belongs to God in the highest degree.

FUN ACTIVITY FOR CHILDREN

This activity is best done with a group of at least four people who know each other pretty well. It's a good activity for the whole family to play!

Each person should write on small pieces of paper five things that would be a part of his or her perfect day. Examples might be 'going to the beach' or 'playing with my dog' or perhaps 'taking a long nap.' Each person will have unique things that would make for their perfect day.

Next, choose one person to begin the game. This person chooses another person and tries to guess one of the items on his or her list. If the guess is correct, this person takes that piece of paper from the other player and can make another guess of the same or a different player. When someone guesses incorrectly, the person who was chosen gets to make a guess of someone else. When all five of a player's items are guessed they're out of the game. When only one person is left in the game, that's the winner!

As always, it's recommended that a discussion follow relating the game to this particular lesson.

OUTSIDE ADVENTURE

Let's go outside and compare our current circumstances to what we might be able to imagine heaven to be like. For each of the categories, each person should give a rating between 1 (horrible) to 10 (perfect). Once finished add up each of their lists and see how close each is to a perfect score of 40, which would indicate perfect happiness in mind and body.

1. How would you rate the nature, scenery, and weather around you on a scale of 1-10? Is it the most beautiful (10) you've ever experienced or is it the most unpleasant (1) ever?

2. How do you feel physically? Do you have a stomach ache or pains anywhere? Are you tired or energetic? Hungry or thirsty or perfectly satisfied in every way? Rate It from 1-10.

3. How is your mood? Are you joyful or sad? Enthusiastic or anxious? Rate it from 1-10.

4. How well do you think you know God in a personal way? Do you know everything possible about Him (10) or you feel like you know nothing about Him (1) at all? (This is a bit of a trick question because in this life we can never have a 10 for this category)

AWE AND WONDER

Consider the things we do just about every moment of every day in order to bring about our own personal happiness. When we begin feeling the pangs of hunger or thirst, we normally find the food or drink that will relieve us of these physical desires. We wear appropriate clothes because we want to have the greatest level of comfort possible. When we get sick, we see the doctor or sometimes take the proper medicine or therapy to begin feeling better. When we get tired, we find a place to rest our bodies.

All these things bring us some degree of happiness, but they're never permanent fixes. Don't the hunger and thirst and sleepiness return? There is only one true happiness and it is God Himself. Think about what St. Thomas wrote above, that God is happiness, and that some creatures—though not all—are able to participate in this perfect happiness through an operation of their intellect. Isn't it exciting to consider that you and I are such creatures who are able to truly experience God in the fullest?

PRAYER

My God, I desire You as my perfect happiness, the Creator and source of all that I desire. You are my Truth, my Goodness and my Beauty. Please allow me to know You as best I can here on earth and give me the grace to enjoy You perfectly one day in heaven.

LESSON 22

How Are The Persons of the Trinity Related to Each Other?

Now that we've learned a lot about God, His attributes and how He is our perfect Beatitude, we'll learn in this lesson a way in which we are like Him. Sure, we're made to His image and likeness, created with intellect and will, but how else are we like Him? Here we learn that in God there is a community of persons, three in one. The Father, Son and Holy Spirit are known as The Trinity. Each of the three persons has a relationship with the other. This is what it means to say that there are 'relations' in God. And while we likely can't relate personally to some of God's qualities, such as Him being all-perfect or all-powerful or all-knowing, we can certainly relate to having relations because it's a big part of our daily lives. After all, we all have many relations (or relationships) with family members and friends and neighbors and countless other people every day.

The key here is to understand that God is not a loner God. Rather, His very essence is one of relationship between persons, and the Persons of the Trinity share one divine nature. While all creatures have relation to other creatures (a dog has relations with another dog, for example), only those with intellectual natures (God, angels and humans) can relate to each other in a personal way. That's why we're called 'persons' as we'll learn more about in the next lesson.

ST. THOMAS SAYS...

Relation in its own proper meaning signifies only what refers to another. Such regard to another exists sometimes in the nature of things, as in those things which by their own very nature are ordered to each other, and have a mutual inclination; and such relations are necessarily real relations....But when something proceeds from a principle of the same nature, then both the one proceeding and the source of procession, agree in the same order; and then they have real relations to each other. Therefore as the divine processions are in the identity of the same nature, these relations according to the divine processions, are necessarily real relations.

FUN ACTIVITY FOR CHILDREN

Let's have each child draw his or her own family tree. He or she should draw himself or herself on the bottom of a piece of paper and his siblings either to the right or left depending on age. Above he or she should draw or write the names of his or her parents, and above the parents should be the name of the parents' parents (the child's grandparents). Let's go one level higher and draw or write the names of their great-grandparents (his or her parents' grandparents).

Once this is completed, the child should sit down with his or her parents and ask about all of these people. Write down some of their best qualities and characteristics as remembered by the parents. Were they patient, funny, good story-tellers, hardworking, serious?

Hopefully this activity will be the catalyst for a great discussion about relationships within an extended family, and the memories that are passed down from one generation to the next. In light of this, why do they think it's important that God be a communion of persons that have relationships with each other?

OUTSIDE ADVENTURE

Go outside with a notepad and spend some time observing and making note of all the relationships you see during your time outside. This will require you to be very observant of the various creatures you encounter and how they are interacting with one another. For example, you might see a bee flying around a flower garden looking for nectar. Write down 'bee' and 'flower' and note their relationship. If you see two dogs playing, write it down and note the nature of the relationship. Maybe you see two people talking or laughing. Write it down. The key here is to practice becoming more aware of the relational nature of our world, not only with human beings but with all creatures. Everywhere we look we see relationships. It's part of life and a big part of our world. Try to make a connection between this adventure, what you've written down and the main point of this particular lesson.

AWE AND WONDER

Do you remember in the first lesson of this book it was explained that some of the Truths we receive from God exceed the capacity of our natural reason? It was explained that these truths, or mysteries are called Sacred Doctrine. One such example is the Most Holy Trinity, the most fundamental Truth and Mystery of our Christian faith. How are we to understand three Persons in one God? We can find in Holy Scripture nearly thirty explicit references to there being only one God and this is a fundamental teaching of our Christian faith. But at the same time we read of the Father saying, 'This is my chosen Son: Listen to Him.' (Luke 9:35) and Jesus clearly speaks about and to His Father in Scripture, as when He says, 'My Father, if it is not possible that this cup pass without my drinking it, your will be done.' (Matthew 26:42). And at another time Jesus says, 'I will ask the Father and He will give you another Advocate, the Spirit of Truth.' (John 14:16). Perhaps we've heard of this great mystery since we were children and we no longer ponder just how bewildering, how mysterious it is to wrap our minds around three Persons in One God.

PRAYER

My God, there are things I do not fully understand, such as the teaching on the Most Holy Trinity, but I accept these teachings with faith. Please increase my faith so that I will better understand who You are as three persons in one God.

LESSON 23

What Does It Mean To Be A Person?

How would you answer this question—what is a person? We just learned that there are three Persons in the Blessed Trinity and you likely know that you're a person. In fact, only a person is capable of reading this book! It's a word we use often, without perhaps giving too much thought about what it means. Even a child likely knows that his dog or cat or pet turtle is not a person, but they know that their friends at school and their siblings and mom and dad and Uncle Bob and Aunt Sally are all persons. And they know there is a big difference between Uncle Bob and their pet turtle or dog. But what exactly is it?

Only persons have what St. Thomas calls 'dominion' over their actions. This means persons make decisions and can do good and evil, and can be held accountable for the choices they make. And most importantly, only persons can achieve the Beatific Vision, which means only they are able to see (and know) God in His essence. And recall we learned in a previous lesson that only rational, intellectual beings can conceive of 'ideas.' St. Thomas defines a person as a 'substance' that is 'rational' or 'intellectual.' You'll see below that St. Thomas defines a 'substance' as something that is individual, having a distinct identity. Being a person is a trait we share with the angels and the Persons of the Most Blessed Trinity but not with the animals, because they don't have rational souls. So as much as we may care about our pet dog or cat or bird, we must understand that there is a big difference between them and us in regard to our nature and our final end.

ST. THOMAS SAYS...

Although the universal and particular exist in every genus, nevertheless, in a certain special way, the individual belongs to the genus of substance. For substance is individualized by itself…

Further still, in a more special and perfect way, the particular and the individual are found in the rational substances which have dominion over their own actions; and which are not only made to act, like others; but which can act of themselves; for actions belong to singulars. Therefore, also the individuals of the rational nature have a special name even among other substances; and this name is 'person.'

Thus the term 'individual substance' is placed in the definition of person, as signifying the singular in the genus of substance; and the term 'rational nature' is added, as signifying the singular in rational substances.

FUN ACTIVITY FOR CHILDREN

If you're familiar with the old 'Duck, Duck,Goose!' game, you'll know how to play this game. Get everyone in a circle and have one child go around the outside of the circle, lightly tapping one person on the head at a time. When tapping each person, the child should say the name of a person, such as 'Aunt Sally' or 'Abraham Lincoln' or 'St. Therese of Lisieux' or even names of people familiar with everyone playing. The child should continue around the circle doing this, but at some point he or she will tap a person and say the name of an irrational creature such as 'turtle' or 'elephant,' etc. When this happens the one who was tapped stands up and tries to catch the child before he or she runs all the way around the circle and back to the second child's place in the circle. If the child is caught before getting to the place, they must try again. If they return to the spot before getting caught, the second child then goes around the circle as did the first child.

Keep in mind that angels are persons so these will be allowed in the game!

Be sure to talk about how this game relates to the topic of the lesson. Does everyone understand the difference between a person and a non-person?

OUTSIDE ADVENTURE

Let's go out on a scavenger hunt in our yard or a nearby park! Parents, you select the outdoor location for the hunt and then prepare a list of ten Items that are likely to be found where you are, such as an acorn, a pine cone, a piece of bark, a leaf from a tree, and perhaps even some live creatures like an earthworm, an ant or a cricket. Use your imagination and see what kind of a list you can create for the children.

Next, either make copies of the list of items or have the

kids write down the names of each item on the list. See who can go out and find and bring back all of the items on the list.

What's the connection between this scavenger hunt and this lesson on persons? Well, if you're able to play this game, you're a person! Because only a person can read and only a person can understand the 'idea' of the items that are on the list and be able to go out and find them and bring them back.

The point is that we do many simple things every day which no other creatures can do, because we are rational substances with intellectual natures. Isn't it great to be a person!

AWE AND WONDER

St. Thomas Aquinas defines a person as an individual substance of rational nature. We know that we are persons because we're reading this, as was mentioned above. But one of the big debates in our culture is when does personhood begin? When does a substance become a person? This happens at the moment of conception, when a rational soul enters the forming body inside the mother's womb. But there seems to be a problem here. St. Thomas says a person has 'dominion over their own actions' and can 'act of themselves.' Certainly a new human, an embryo or zygote, can't do this, right? Christian theologians explain that a person is also one who is able to grow into the ability to perform such personal acts. A cat or monkey or lizard embryo will never grow into a person.

But a human embryo will. Therefore, such a tiny substance is already a person.

PRAYER

My God, thank You for blessing me with personhood, and thank You for allowing me to have reason and free will and to be able to choose to love You. Please protect me from ever abusing this privilege.

LESSON 24

Why Do We Call The Son The 'Word?'

We all know what 'words' are because we use them all the time. In this lesson we'll learn why the Son of God is often referred to as 'the Word,' and how this can be explained through our own experience with the words that we speak every day. Be warned that this is a difficult concept to grasp, so be patient. It may be necessary to read this section a few times to make sure it makes sense. The challenging part is trying to understand that God's essence (what He is) and His understanding are the same thing, which means that for God to be and to understand are not different. God the Father conceives of the eternal 'Word' (the Son) within the Trinity, while the two remain one Being (God).

We exist and have an essence, but we also understand things with our intellects. These are all separate in us, and this is one of the reasons that we are a lot more complicated than God, Who is perfectly simple. So, when God the Father generates the Son as His 'Word,' there is nothing happening outside the Trinity, because to understand and to generate a 'Word' are parts of the very essence of God. With us, understanding is separate from our essence. We are not our understanding; rather, it's just one of the many things we do. But with God, they're one and the same thing. Does that make sense? I hope so!

ST. THOMAS SAYS...

Word said of God in its proper sense, is used personally, and is the proper name of the person of the Son. For it signifies an emanation of the intellect: and the person Who proceeds in God, by way of emanation of the intellect, is called the Son; and this procession is called generation. Hence it follows that the Son alone is properly called Word in God. "To be" and "to understand" are not the same in us. Hence that which in us has intellectual being does not belong to our nature. But in God "to be" and "to understand" are one and the same: hence the Word of God is not an accident in Him, or an effect of His; but belongs to His very nature.

FUN ACTIVITY FOR CHILDREN

This activity will test the child's memory and highlight an important aspect of this lesson as well. Have one child write down ten words on a piece of paper. The words should be generic nouns such as 'hippopotamus,' 'airplane' and 'mansion,' and not specific nouns like 'Albert Einstein' or 'George Washington.' Once the ten words have been written down, the child who wrote them should slowly read his list out loud twice for all to hear. The other child or children who are playing are then to see how many of the words they can remember, and then write them down on their own piece of paper. It's not necessary the words be in exact order. After the children have written down as many words as they can remember, you can check to see if their words are correct.

121

In light of this lesson on the 'Word' of God, talk about how these words first entered the mind of the first child as concepts, then ended up on paper, then were spoken, and then the same concept entered into the other children's minds as well. Their 'words' were transferred from one mind to the other!

How might this be a good activity to help learn more about the second Person of the Trinity as the 'Word of God?'

OUTSIDE ADVENTURE

Get a pad of sketch paper and a pack of multi-colored pencils, and find the most scenic spot you can find near where you live. Hopefully it's a spot where you can sit down with your pad and pencils, and see a good representation of God's beauty as expressed through His created world. Ideally there would be some water like a pond or creek (or maybe even the ocean!) along with trees and hopefully even some animals as well.

Now do your best to draw this scene being as specific as possible. While drawing, pay attention to the details of your drawing and how when you first observe something with your eyes, it becomes a concept in your mind, and then you put this concept on paper in the form of your art work. Be sure to pay attention to the distinction between yourself and the concepts and art you are creating.

Once finished, observe the whole picture and see how you can both observe individual features of your picture, and you can also observe the picture as a whole, in one glance. Talk about how this relates to this particular lesson.

AWE AND WONDER

Normally when we think of the 'Word of God' (as in the Second Person of the Holy Trinity), we think of Jesus as a human being walking the earth some 2,000 years ago. What we want to ponder now is that the 'Word' of God existed long before Jesus ever came to be born into the world at Bethlehem. The Word of God is the concept in the 'mind' of God the Father, and this concept has existed for all of eternity. In other words, the Word of God was never created. He was generated by the Father but not in time. The Word existed long before (for eternity in fact) He became man and walked the earth as Jesus Christ. So let us ponder the Son, the Word, not in the flesh for now (that will come later), but as the invisible intelligible concept of the Father. Reflect on this mystery and be filled with awe for God!

PRAYER

Dear God, please give me the grace to understand the Second Person of the Most Holy Trinity as the uncreated Word of the Father, generated eternally from the Father as the uncreated Son of God.

LESSON 25

Why Is "Love' A Name For The Holy Spirit?

Everyone can relate to the word 'love.' We all 'love' things and we love people, and we either are loved in return or wish to be loved. But it's also true that in the English language the word 'love' is used too generally. We speak of loving God and our parents and our friends, but we also often speak of how much we 'love' pizza and sleeping in on Saturday mornings and going to parties. So how is it that the Third Person of the Most Holy Trinity is called 'Love?'

Scripture tells us that 'God is love,' which refers to the Blessed Trinity as a whole. In this lesson, we learn that the Holy Spirit in particular, as a unique Person within the Trinity, is called 'Love.' We have already shown how the Word is generated through God's intellect and understanding of Himself.

Here we consider how God has not only intellect but also will, or intellectual desire, and it is through the Father and Son's will that love (or the Holy Spirit) results (proceeds) eternally. So, the love between the Father and the Son through an act of the Divine Will means that the Holy Spirit proceeds from them as Love itself.

ST. THOMAS SAYS...

There are two processions in God, one by way of the intellect, which is the procession of the Word, and another by way of the will, which is the procession of Love.... For as when a thing is understood by anyone, there results in the one who understands a conception of the object understood, which conception we call word; so when anyone loves an object, a certain impression results, so to speak, of the thing loved in the affection of the lover; by reason of which the object loved is said to be in the lover; as also the thing understood is in the one who understands; so that when anyone understands and loves himself he is in himself, not only by real identity, but also as the object understood is in the one who understands, and the thing loved is in the lover.

FUN ACTIVITY FOR CHILDREN

Get a plain white T-shirt that you don't mind getting marked up and some fabric markers of various colors. You're going to make this into your 'Love Shirt' to remind you of all the things you love and to which you are attracted.

Start by either writing the word 'God' on the top front of the shirt or drawing some symbol for Him in its place.

Next, fill up the shirt with names and art by having everyone you love sign it with their name or some kind of drawing. You can also draw on your shirt all the things you 'love' such as your favorite foods and drinks, your favorite sports teams or pictures to represent your hobbies or anything else that you love, like your favorite books or movies.

Once this is complete you will literally have all of the things you love on you as a part of you.

Talk about how this relates to the quote by St. Thomas above, where he says that when one loves something a 'certain impression' results of the loved thing on the lover.

OUTSIDE ADVENTURE

Let's have a treasure hunt! Divide your group into two teams with equal numbers of children. Each team should put together a 'treasure' for the other team made up of things they love, such as edible treats, candy, toys or whatever they would really like. Next, put the treasures in a paper bag or shoe box or some other kind of container. Now, one team at a time goes outside and hides their treasure in a place where it will be safe for a while and not in open view. Once the first team is finished, the second team should do the same, hiding their treasure in a separate place.

Next, each team should make a treasure map of the neighborhood which will provide clues as to the whereabouts of their treasure. Once both teams have finished their maps, it's time to exchange maps and let the two teams go outside and try to find the other team's treasures. See which team can find their treasure first.

See if you can make the connection between this activity and the lesson taught here about the Holy Spirit. Focus on the attitude the team has about their hidden treasure when they are trying to find it. Think about their desire, their 'love' for this unknown secret that awaits them! Have fun!

AWE AND WONDER

We often think of the Holy Spirit as a dove or a light or some other symbol that is used in Scripture. But let's now consider the Holy Spirit as fire, a burning fire of love between the Father and the Son. Most of us have experienced a burning desire for something or a burning love for a person. And we know how powerful it can be. In fact, it can become so ardent that it's difficult to think of anything else, while our desire burns for this particular thing or person.

Just imagine the intensity of the love of God! And this love is so strong that we give it a name: the Holy Spirit, Love itself. God generously gives of this Love (the Holy Spirit) when we are baptized, and we are strengthened in this Love of the Holy Spirit at Confirmation. What do you think we could accomplish in our spiritual lives if we allowed this Love to be unleashed in our hearts?

PRAYER

Holy Spirit, burning Love of the Father and the Son, please inflame in me a desire for God and for the salvation of souls.

LESSON 26

Why Is The Holy Spirit Called 'Gift?'

We've learned that the Father generates the Son as the eternal Word and the Holy Spirit results in the love between the Father and the Son. Next, let's learn one more name for the Holy Spirit. It's a word that will instantly bring a smile to anyone's face, because we all love to receive (and give) them. The Holy Spirit is a 'Gift' from God intended only for rational creatures like you and me.

Recall that in the first lesson, we learned that we need help from God to achieve our final end, and in a later lesson our final end was given a name: Beatitude, which is perfect happiness and God Himself. Recall we learned also that an intellectual nature distinguishes a person from a non-person. Only persons can come to know God, to love Him, and ultimately rest with Him in heaven. And since we cannot earn the right to rest with God for eternity by our own power, we accept it as something undeserved, and therefore it's called a gift…from God to us. The gift God give us is Himself!

ST. THOMAS SAYS...

The word "gift" imports an aptitude for being given. And what is given has an aptitude or relation both to the giver and to that to which it is given. For it would not be given by anyone, unless it was his to give; and it is given to someone to be his. But we are said to possess what we can freely use or enjoy as we please: and in this way a divine person cannot be possessed, except by a rational creature united to God. Other creatures can be moved by a divine person, not, however, in such a way as to be able to enjoy the divine person, and to use the effect thereof. The rational creature does sometimes attain thereto; as when it is made partaker of the divine Word and of the Love proceeding, so as freely to know God truly and to love God rightly. Hence the rational creature alone can possess the divine person. Nevertheless in order that it may possess Him in this manner, its own power avails nothing: hence this must be given it from above; for that is said to be given to us which we have from another source. Thus a divine person can "be given," and can be a "gift."

FUN ACTIVITY FOR CHILDREN

Let's play a game of charades based on the theme of this lesson. Have each person playing the game write down the name of five irrational animals (creatures other than human beings, like dogs, spiders, porcupines, etc.) and the name of five specific human beings (Abraham Lincoln, Amelia Earhart, St. Joseph, etc.) on small pieces of paper and then fold each piece of paper a couple of times. Once everyone has done this, put all the pieces of paper in a basket or hat or something that can hold the entries for the game.

Now, choose the order that you are going to go and let the first person go up, draw one of the pieces of paper and act it out without using words or any noises at all. Everyone else can guess which animal or human being is being acted out. Time out a minute for each child and see how many they can have correctly guessed during that time. When a minute has elapsed, let the next child do the same until all the clues have been guessed correctly. You can award a point system if you'd like to make it a competition!

After the activity, have a discussion about the difference between acting out the irrational animals and acting out the human beings and what the biggest differences were in deciding how to act out each of them during the game.

OUTSIDE ADVENTURE

So far in all of the previous lessons, we've learned a lot about how the created world, including the various creatures that inhabit it, are blessings from God. We know also that we can learn about our great God by simply being more observant of our surroundings. It's not difficult to see these creatures as gifts from a loving God.

During this activity, let's change things around a bit by offering gifts to the very creatures that have blessed our lives. Be creative and think of what gifts you can offer different creatures near where you live. Perhaps you can offer some bread crumbs to the ducks in a nearby lake, or put a feeder out in your backyard for other species of birds, like hummingbirds, for example. You can give your own or a neighbors' dog or cat a nice treat (with the neighbor's permission, of course!), either something edible or a nice petting or some play time. How about leaving a sugar cube in a nearby field to make some ants' day! Be creative and think of other similar gifts you can offer.

Take notice while doing this that none of the gifts you are offering are of an intellectual nature. You can't give these creatures books or cards or your favorite movie, right? While this may sound like an odd observation, it connects well to this lesson. How so?

AWE AND WONDER

Have you ever heard of the word 'species' as related to humans, animals and plants? Do you know what the word means? Species is defined most simply as a group of living organisms consisting of similar individuals.

Okay, the next question is—do you know to which species you belong? (Homo sapiens)

Do you know how many species of animals, plants and insects exist in the world today? (The truth is no one knows for sure, but the best estimates are that there are as many as 8.7 million different species of

131

creatures in the world. That's 8,700,000 species each of which would account for millions if not billions of individual creatures.)

How many of the 8.7 million species of creatures are capable of receiving the gift of the Holy Spirit from God?

Only one. Homo sapiens. That's you and me!

PRAYER

My God, thank You for loving me so much as to give me the gift of your Holy Spirit, and allowing me to possess your Divine Nature. Please give me the grace to accept this gift with humility and gratitude.

LESSON 27

Is God The End Of All Things?

A recurring theme of the Summa is our being both created by and called back to a loving God. Our lives are like a boomerang in that sense: exit and return. In theology, the study of the end is called teleology. Each of our actions is done for a purpose and is directed toward an end. We eat to relieve hunger and drink to relieve our thirst. We work to earn money for our expenses, and we press the accelerator of the car so that the car will move. Everything has an end, and each small end in our daily lives is moving us toward a bigger end, which in turn moves us toward an even bigger or more important end. So, what is the final end to which all the other little ends lead? In a word, it's God, our Beatitude.

Everything we do, every decision we make, is an attraction to something we love. All our little 'loves' are designed to lead us to a final big 'Love,' which is our Creator. God made us in such a way that we are naturally drawn to our own perfection, our own goodness, and all of this directs us right back to Him from Whom we came. In a sense, we are programmed by God to return back to Him. But unlike the ducks flying south or the salmon swimming upstream, we have been given free will, and with it the ability to rebel against this gentle Divine tug.

ST. THOMAS SAYS...

Every agent acts for an end: otherwise one thing would not follow more than another from the action of the agent, unless it were by chance. Now the end of the agent and of the patient considered as such is the same, but in a different way respectively. For the impression which the agent intends to produce, and which the patient intends to receive, are one and the same. Some things, however, are both agent and patient at the same time: these are imperfect agents, and to these it belongs to intend, even while acting, the acquisition of something. But it does not belong to the First Agent, Who is agent only, to act for the acquisition of some end; He intends only to communicate His perfection, which is His goodness; while every creature intends to acquire its own perfection, which is the likeness of the divine perfection and goodness. Therefore the divine goodness is the end of all things.

FUN ACTIVITY FOR CHILDREN

This activity is best done with a larger group, preferably at least six if possible.

One person per game will decide to be the reader and facilitator rather than a player. All the other players will secretly write down on a small piece of paper the name of some specific creature, like a tomato plant or blue jay or orangutan, for example. Next, all the pieces of paper will be given to the facilitator who then reads all of the individual creatures' names two times only in the same order. The facilitator then chooses someone to begin the game.

The person chosen tried to connect one of the animals to one of the players. For example, 'Mary, are you the pumpkin?' If this person guesses correctly, Mary becomes a part of his or her team and the two, as a team, try to guess someone else's creature. If correct, that person also joins the team but if Incorrect, that person gets to make a guess of their own from either that same person or another player. The game is over when someone has accumulated everyone else onto his or her team.

After the game, the facilitator again can read all of the names of the creatures, and all can have a conversation about how these creatures act for an end and how also the divine goodness is their end, as mentioned above by St. Thomas.

OUTSIDE ADVENTURE

Let's do a very simple lesson to highlight the main point from this lesson, namely that all things act for an end. It's clear that we are acting for an end. Everything we do has a purpose and as we've seen, ultimately our purpose is to be with God and know Him perfectly.

Go to the gardening section of a store and get a packet of seeds of one or more popular vegetables, such as beans, snap peas, cucumbers and tomatoes. If you don't already have the following, be sure to get them: paper towels and a clear glass jar. Next, begin pushing sheets of the paper towel into the jar until the jar is filled. Put water into the jar to get the towels damp. Push the towels down and then put more towels and water into the jar until it's filled. The towels should be damp but not soaking wet. Next, put your various seeds along the sides of the jar so that they are visible. Put the jar outside in direct sunlight if the temperature is warm enough or on a window sill or under a light if it's too cold outside.

Now, keep an eye on the various seeds to see them begin to open up and grow into seedlings. Notice how each 'knows' what it's to do and what it is to become. Would you say that even a seed is acting for an end?

AWE AND WONDER

St. Thomas says that "every agent acts for an end." By 'agent' he means all creatures, such as plants, insects, birds, reptiles, humans, and the angels. Another way of saying this is that everything in God's creation has a purpose. Life is not random but ordered, and things happen for a reason. All animals act for a purpose even if they don't understand what it is. Recall in the opening paragraph it was observed that we are 'always on the move.' In some cases it's accurate to say creatures are being moved. The bird flies to find food for her chicks because without this the baby birds would die. The snake hibernates and the ducks fly south in the winter. In an exceptional way, our lives have meaning and each of our actions has a purpose and is helping to lead us to an end. Our loving Father calls His children home to eternal happiness. We need

136

only obey and respond to Him by aligning our will to His perfect will.

PRAYER

My God, thank You for creating in me a natural desire to rest in You. Please provide for me the grace to always seek You and to make decisions consistent with reaching my final end.

LESSON 28

Are All Creatures Like God?

So far we've learned about the various creatures that God has created, such as lifeless things (like rocks and mountains) and irrational animals (like hyenas and parrots and monkeys). In the last lesson we focused on irrational creatures such as oak trees and sparrows, crickets and ants and puppies and fish. We practiced a 'spirituality of awareness' in connecting each of these beautiful creatures to their ultimate cause, our great God.

Now we learn how each of these not only draws us to God but that each also is like God Himself. Every creature has at least a 'trace' of God, because each reveals some quality of the Divine Being. The highest of all visible creatures in our world, without a doubt, is the human person. Endowed with intellect, will and a body capable of expressing ourselves to others, each person is a most beautiful representation of Almighty God who is pure Spirit, intellect and will. The human person can conceive of ideas, reflecting the relationship between the Father and the Son. A human can love and be loved, reflecting the person of the Holy Spirit as the love between the Father and Son. But all creatures in some way, large and small, are beautiful reflections of God.

ST. THOMAS SAYS...

Every effect in some degree represents its cause, but diversely. For some effects represent only the causality of the cause, but not its form; as smoke represents fire. Such a representation is called a "trace", for a trace shows that someone has passed by but not who it is. Other effects represent the cause as regards the similitude of its form, as fire generated represents fire generating; and a statue of Mercury represents Mercury....In rational creatures, possessing intellect and will, there is found the representation of the Trinity by way of image, inasmuch as there is found in them the word conceived, and the love proceeding.

FUN ACTIVITY FOR CHILDREN

Let's call this activity 'stick figure drawing fun!' Have a first child write down the names of five generic creatures or created things (such as bird, fish, chair, cloud, etc.) but keep the list a secret for now. Next, he or she will draw stick figures of the words, one at a time, on paper. The goal is to have the drawing identified by another person as quickly as possible. Once the first drawing is guessed correctly, the child moves on to the second and third, etc., until all have been guessed correctly by anyone who is playing the game. Time how fast the child can have all five of the stick figure drawings identified. Once finished, the next child can do the same, and the first child joins the group trying to guess the drawings. See who can be the fastest and who can identify the most drawings.

When finished, have a fun discussion about 'ideas' (as learned in a previous lesson). Recall how when a stick figure of a cat or tree is identified, the 'idea' is of all cats, all trees. Catness, treeness is expressed. Discuss also how only rational creatures (like us) can conceive of ideas and how this makes us more 'like God' than the irrational creatures.

OUTSIDE ADVENTURE

In most of our outdoor adventures so far we've focused on God's creatures that do not share our gift of humanity. We've marveled at the beauty of birds and flowers and countless other amazing creatures. Today, however, we're going to focus our attention on our fellow human beings, and hopefully we'll begin to see them in a way we've never considered before.

Go outside to a place such as a park or some other location where you will likely encounter a lot of people. If possible and safe, you could go to a place where you will see the downtrodden and the homeless. As you observe them, consider what the Catechism of the Catholic Church says (CCC 460)—that 'the Word became flesh to make us (human beings) 'partakers of the divine nature.' St. Athanasius, a Doctor of the Church, went so far as to teach that 'the Son of God became man so that we might become God.' And St. Thomas Aquinas adds that the Son of God so much wants us to share in His divinity that He, Who was

140

made man, might 'make men gods.' We are not God, of course, and we are not divine, but being made to God's image and likeness, the human person is the creature that you will encounter today who most beautifully and closely resembles God. How can this change the way you see and treat every person you meet today?

AWE AND WONDER

Have you worked on changing the way you see the world and the creatures that surround you? Has your daily life become more filled with mystical experiences? Perhaps in the past you looked in a pond and saw a frog or a fish or maybe a snake and that was it. But now hopefully you have reached the point where you can look there and see the hand of God. Without God, these creatures would not exist. God created them and is present in them, holding them in existence, and therefore, they should remind us of His goodness and beauty.

Are you 'seeing God' every day? He's everywhere we look, and most especially in our fellow human beings. Once this new way of seeing the world becomes a habit, everything changes. The lens through which we see the world changes and God begins to 'appear' everywhere. The result of this new 'lens' will be an increase in the experience of joy. Let's spend the rest of our days looking for God and when we find Him, taking time to give Him due praise and honor.

PRAYER

My God, thank You for making Yourself present to me everywhere I look in the world and in the creatures that surround me. Please give me the grace to look for You and find You in all of Your creation.

LESSON 29

Why Are There So Many Different Kinds of Creatures?

Anyone can see that the world is filled with a lot of different kinds of creatures. In fact, a trip to the zoo or the circus or even around your neighborhood is an easy way to witness this fact firsthand. As was mentioned in a previous lesson, there are nearly nine million (9,000,000) different species of animals in the world! But why does there need to be so many different kinds of creatures?

We've learned that God is perfect in every way, and that He possesses the fullness of every goodness and perfection in His very essence. And in His generosity, He has distributed His many qualities and perfections to billions of creatures in the world, so that a variety exists rather than just one. So each creature has some quality that teaches us something about God, but no creature has all of His qualities. If one creature had all of God's qualities, it would be God!

Once we properly understand this, it changes the way we look at the world. We want to begin to see the presence of God in creatures, rather than regarding them just as a science experiment or just something we're sharing, co-existing with in the world. As indicated in a previous lesson, seen properly, all these creatures can be viewed as 'Sacred Veils' of the Divine Essence.

ST. THOMAS SAYS...

The distinction and multitude of things come from the intention of the first agent, who is God. For He brought things into being in order that His goodness might be communicated to creatures, and be represented by them; and because His goodness could not be adequately represented by one creature alone, He produced many and diverse creatures that what was wanting to one in the representation of the divine goodness might be supplied by another. For goodness, which in God is simple and uniform, in creatures is manifold and divided, and hence the whole universe together participates the divine goodness more perfectly, and represents it better than any single creature whatever.

FUN ACTIVITY FOR CHILDREN

This activity helps us be aware of the many different kinds of creatures that inhabit our world. Get into a circle with as many people as would like to play the game and select someone to go first. This person should say the name of any one of God's creatures in the natural world (not made by man) that begins with the letter A. So the first person can say 'Aardvark' or 'Ant' or 'Apricot' for example. Go clockwise around the circle, and each person must say out loud a creature starting with the next letter in the alphabet. The second person says one that begins with the letter B and the third person the letter C, etc. Keep going around as many times as possible, and when you finish the alphabet, begin again with the letter A. When someone either can't think of a creature or repeats one previously mentioned, they are out of the game. The game ends when only one person remains.

Afterwards ask each of the participants to remember one of the creatures that was mentioned during the game and describe what we can come to know about God through this particular creature.

OUTSIDE ADVENTURE

Go to the local store and buy one of the big 64 packs of crayons that come in a variety of colors. Next go to the place near where you live where you will have the greatest variety of colors in the created world. For example, is there a place where you'll likely find leaves of many colors or perhaps soil or flowers of a variety of hues?

Either individually or as a team see how many matches you can make between the colors of the crayons and the colors you see in the natural world. Be as creative as possible and see if you can find lizards or bugs or plants with colors matching the colors of your crayons. You can either do this in a single day, or it can be something that you carry over through the year as the seasons introduce different colors in nature.

Talk about the variety of colors and creatures in the natural world and how this relates to this particular lesson, and how the variety makes it easier for us to come to know God.

AWE AND WONDER

Do you remember the main purpose of the lessons in this book? Isn't it to come to know God as best as we can while here on earth, so that we can prepare to know Him most perfectly one day in the glory of heaven? The amazing teaching of this lesson is that we don't have to wait to get to heaven to begin learning about God or experiencing some aspects of His Goodness. Rather, He has put clues of His beauty, truth, and goodness everywhere we look. We need not look any further than the multitude of creatures that surround us every day, from the gorgeous sunset to a mighty storm to a colorful flower.

In fact, sitting in a room by yourself should be enough to allow you to contemplate God, simply by reflecting on the way He created you. God is everywhere! This should change the way we see the world, and we should never again see any creature in the world as ordinary or mundane.

Do you think a better understanding of this teaching can bring more joy, enthusiasm and meaning to your life? Can our lives be set on fire with wonder by searching for and finding hints of God literally everywhere we look? Does seeing the world this way help us to desire to know God more passionately?

PRAYER

My God, please help me to look for You and find You wherever I go every moment of every day, in Your creatures that surround me.

LESSON 30

Why So Much Inequality Among God's Creatures?

We realize now that the multitude of creatures in the world helps us to understand who God is, because each of them provides a clue about God's nature. But this doesn't explain why some things are so far superior to others. Wouldn't you agree that it's better to be a human than to be a grub worm? And if you couldn't be a human, I bet you'd rather be a mighty lion than plankton floating in the ocean.

So why did God create a world where there is so much inequality? Why can't all things be equal, or why can't there just be fewer creatures in the first place, so that some creatures don't have to be so lowly and seemingly insignificant?

God created the world as a whole that requires many different parts, all of which together create a beautiful mosaic. Each one in its own way contributes to the perfection of the whole. And this perfection requires that some be superior to others and some therefore must be inferior.

ST. THOMAS SAYS...

It is part of the best agent to produce an effect which is best in its entirety; but this does not mean that He makes every part of the whole the best absolutely, but in proportion to the whole; in the case of an animal, for instance, its goodness would be taken away if every part of it had the dignity of an eye. Thus, therefore, God also made the universe to be best as a whole, according to the mode of a creature; whereas He did not make each single creature best, but one better than another....Inequality comes from the perfection of the whole. This appears also in works done by art; for the roof of a house differs from the foundation, not because it is made of other material; but in order that the house may be made perfect of different parts, the artificer seeks different material; indeed, he would make such material if he could.

FUN ACTIVITY FOR CHILDREN

See if you can round up at least five children to put on a play for the parents or other adults or siblings interested in attending. Decide who is going to do the following roles for the play: the actors, the director, the set designers, the artists for making and distributing tickets and promotional materials, and the writers of the play. Make sure everyone has a role and that there is someone responsible for filling all or most of these assignments.

Now get busy writing the play, working on the set, the promotional materials, the tickets and the practice. Work together as a group to put on as good a play as possible. When you're ready, invite the parents, other adults and siblings to purchase tickets to see the play.

When you're finished, talk about how important the various roles and responsibilities were in putting on a successful play. How important was it that everyone did their part for the play to be a success? Were some roles more important than others? What if everyone wanted to be an actor or a writer or a director of the play? What if one of the other roles had been unfilled? How would that have impacted the success of the play?

Finally, talk about how this activity relates to this lesson.

OUTSIDE ADVENTURE

In this final activity of the first book in the St. Thomas Aquinas for Everyone series, we're going to go outside and see if we can find what many would consider very insignificant creatures in the natural world.

Go out in your back yard or a nearby creek or field, somewhere close by where you will be able to see a variety of life. Bring a jar or can in which you can put anything you catch.

Have a contest to see who can find the 'most insignificant' creature. Lift up logs or rocks to see what you might find. Being careful not to pick up any creatures that can hurt you, see if you can place in your jar what you'd consider the simplest and least important creatures. Perhaps it's a tiny bug or a blade of grass. See what you can find and be creative!

When everyone comes back together, have all compare what they've found. See if you can do some research on the creatures you've found to find out what is their purpose in the 'big picture.' See if you can determine if there are in fact any creatures that are totally insignificant or if they all do play a role, even a small one, in God's big plan.

AWE AND WONDER

In a previous lesson we learned to be in awe of the simplest of creatures that God has created, such as a common housefly or a gnat or a mosquito. Each of these little bugs is so intricately designed with complicated systems of blood flow and digestion and aerodynamics, that it can inspire great awe in us, if we allow ourselves to stop and be amazed at the perfection and design God has put into each creature. In fact, these little bugs live very short lives, and their biggest purpose in life may be to be food for other larger animals. Some creatures have very short life spans, like the housefly that normally lives less than a month and a mayfly that will be lucky to live even 24 hours! Considering that God puts so much detail and concern into the creation of such seemingly lowly creatures, how much more concern and interest do you think He put into creating you and other fellow human beings who are made to His image and likeness? Isn't it incredible to know that this God we've learned so much about in these lessons, designed us to be exactly who we are, and that He loves us intensely and desires to spend eternity with us?

PRAYER

My God, please help me to stop and see the value and significance of every one of Your creatures in light of the perfection You have designed for the whole of creation.

ABOUT THE AUTHOR

Dave Palmer lives in Texas with his wife, Paula, and their three children. He earned a Masters degree in Theology from the University of Dallas, and has spent the past ten years studying and teaching the theology and philosophy of St. Thomas Aquinas to young people, through online courses and religious education classes at his parish. He serves as the Executive Director of the Guadalupe Radio Network's Catholic radio station in north Texas. He has a passion for helping people of all ages better know, love and desire God more passionately through a deeper understanding of St. Thomas Aquinas' masterpiece, the *Summa Theologica*.

Summma Theologica Citations in
St. Thomas Aquinas For Everyone

1. *Summa Theologica* Part 1, Question 1, Article 1, Corpus
2. *Summa Theologica* Part 1, Question 1, Article 9, Corpus
3. *Summa Theologica* Part 1, Question 2, Article 2, Corpus
4. *Summa Theologica* Part 1, Question 2, Article 3, Corpus
5. *Summa Theologica* Part 1, Question 3, Article 7, Corpus
6. *Summa Theologica* Part 1, Question 4, Article 2, Corpus
7. *Summa Theologica* Part 1, Question 5, Article 3, Corpus & Reply to Objection 2
8. *Summa Theologica* Part 1, Question 5, Article 4, Corpus
9. *Summa Theologica* Part 1, Question 8, Article 2, Corpus
10. *Summa Theologica* Part 1, Question 9, Article 1, Corpus
11. *Summa Theologica* Part 1, Question 10, Article 2, Corpus
12. *Summa Theologica* Part 1, Question 12, Article 1, Corpus
13. *Summa Theologica* Part 1, Question 12, Article 6, Corpus
14. *Summa Theologica* Part 1, Question 13, Article 11, Corpus
15. *Summa Theologica* Part 1, Question 14, Article 8, Corpus
16. *Summa Theologica* Part 1, Question 15, Article 1, Corpus
17. *Summa Theologica* Part 1, Question 19, Article 6, Corpus
18. *Summa Theologica* Part 1, Question 20, Article 3, Corpus
19. *Summa Theologica* Part 1, Question 22, Article 2, Corpus
20. *Summa Theologica* Part 1, Question 22, Article 4, Corpus
21. *Summa Theologica* Part 1, Question 26, Article 1, Corpus
22. *Summa Theologica* Part 1, Question 28, Article 1, Corpus
23. *Summa Theologica* Part 1, Question 29, Article 1, Corpus
24. *Summa Theologica* Part 1, Question 34, Article 2, Corpus & Reply to Objection 1
25. *Summa Theologica* Part 1, Question 37, Article 1, Corpus
26. *Summa Theologica* Part 1, Question 38, Article 1, Corpus
27. *Summa Theologica* Part 1, Question 44, Article 4, Corpus
28. *Summa Theologica* Part 1, Question 45, Article 7, Corpus
29. *Summa Theologica* Part 1, Question 47, Article 1, Corpus
30. *Summa Theologica* Part 1, Question 47, Article 2, Reply to Objections 1 & 3

Made in the USA
Monee, IL
31 March 2021